T0197095

FORTITUDE

THE STORY OF MY ANCESTORS

CHARLES E. MITCHELL RENTSCHLER

authorHOUSE®

AuthorHouse™
1663 Liberty Drive
Bloomington, IN 47403
www.authorhouse.com
Phone: 1 (800) 839-8640

Published by AuthorHouse   12/20/2018

ISBN: 978-1-5462-2773-1 (sc)
ISBN: 978-1-5462-2771-7 (hc)
ISBN: 978-1-5462-2772-4 (e)

Library of Congress Control Number: 2018902693

Print information available on the last page.

CONTENTS

THE GREAT FLOOD

Jumping its banks was not unusual for the Great Miami River that courses southwest through the Ohio cities of Sidney, Dayton and Hamilton before spilling into the Ohio River just west of Cincinnati. The Miami had flooded eight times in the nineteenth century -- three times since the arrival in Hamilton in 1872 of the author's paternal grandfather, George Adam Rentschler (known as "Adam"), who had come to town as a 26 year-old immigrant from Germany and become one of its most prominent citizens.

But this instance was dramatically different: the rain -- 11" in total – started in Hamilton on Easter Sunday, 1913, and did not quit for three days, and the Miami, which bisected the center of the heavily-industrialized city of 35,000 people, rose from 3' to 35'. AND THAT'S NOT A MISPRINT! The worst weather-event in the state's history, the storm killed 467 people across Ohio -- some 200 in Hamilton alone

The disproportionate loss of life in Hamilton was attributable to a new bridge constructed for the Cincinnati, Hamilton and Dayton Railroad – people then used trains to go any distance (horse-drawn vehicles still out-numbered automobiles in 1913 Hamilton). Built with more gusto than acumen, the CH&D's structure "featured concrete abutments sunk 30' below the bed of the river and a steel span with solid sides 10' high. Until it finally collapsed, the span not only withstood the force of the river, but, with debris piled against its northern side, formed a dam that diverted the current down into the east part of the town," where most of the city's businesses and homes were located. [1]

The tragic demise of their fellow citizens was, of course, the chief concern of Hamiltonians, who quickly gathered and prepared for burial the dead they could find. Then came the job of dealing with the property damage when there was no flood insurance.

Fortunately, Adam hadn't lost any relatives in the flood, but his original and likely most profitable venture, Sohn & Rentschler Foundry, was completely washed away. Additionally, some of his other businesses suffered very serious damage and mucky water was 3' deep in the first floor of his house.

Adam, though, was used to hardship.

---

[1] Flood, March, 1913, Jim Blount, Past/Present Press, 2002

Adam Rentschler (left) and Henry Sohn, partners in
iron foundry celebrate Fourth of July (circa 1895)

1913 flood engulfed the Rentschler home in Hamilton.

Wrecked Buildings of Part of Hooven-Owens & Rentschler Co. during Great Flood March 1913, Hamilton, Ohio.

1913 flood devastated Hooven Owens Rentschler factories in Hamilton

1913 flood waters covered cross-rail on huge milling machine at H.O.R. shop.

1913 flood waters covered cross-rail on huge milling machine at H.O.R. shop.

2

THE ROAD TO HAMILTON

Adam had been born in 1846 in the tiny village of Schmieh, perched atop a mountain 30 miles west of Stuttgart. The youngest of seven children, Adam was 6 years old when his father, Jacob, a wood-cutter struggling to feed his family, decided to stake out a new life in America after his wife's death in 1852. How Jacob raised the money for passage is not known, but the family settled in Newark, New Jersey, surrounded by other German emigres.

Adam attended grade school until he was 11 when his father died. To support himself, he worked in an iron foundry for seven years, taking classes at night. In 1863 at 17 (we suppose, too young to be drafted into the Union Army to fight in the Civil War) Adam married another German immigrant living in Newark, Christine Maria Graff, nicknamed Kate. Producing a son, George Jr., the next year, they moved to Peru, Indiana, in the north-central part of the state to be closer to her parents who, themselves, had emigrated from Germany to a farm near Fulton, twenty miles north. Living in Peru, a railroad town, allowed Adam to commute to work as a foreman of an iron foundry in Indianapolis.

After giving birth to a second son, Henry, in 1866, Kate tragically died aged 22 in 1869. Initially confused what to do with his motherless boys, Adam in 1873 decided to move to Hamilton, Ohio, where the Indianapolis foundry had relocated.

He would take along Henry, now 7, but leave George, 9, with his maternal grandparents in Fulton where he and his future eight sons would spend their lives farming.

For the rest of his life, however, Adam would keep in close touch with his Indiana offspring.

Ohio was no "backwater". In 1870 the geographical center of America's population was 48 miles north-east of Cincinnati and in 1920 it was 15 miles west of Bloomington, Indiana. Upon Adam's arrival, Ohio was the country's third most populous state, and provided seven out of 12 Presidents of the United States during the half-century he lived there. In fact, in the Presidential election of 1920 (the last in Adam's life-time) both candidates came from the Buckeye State – for the Republicans, Warren G. Harding, U.S. Senator, and for the Democrats, James Cox, Governor.

He would remarry a woman from Hamilton and have a second family but only after he had solidly established himself in business.

3

CASHING IN . . . AND OUT

Two years after moving to Hamilton, in 1875, Adam decided he would no longer work for someone else. He started up an iron foundry with $2500 and a partner, Henry Sohn (a bookkeeper for a brewery), and the firm was named Sohn & Rentschler.

Its early years proved extremely difficult, as described decades later in Adam's obituary: "Money was hard to get, orders were slow in coming and young Rentschler traversed the country for miles with horse and buggy soliciting orders. He got a few, at first, but it was hard to realize even enough to pay the small work force . . . In these lean times, young Rentschler after getting the orders would go to the shop, take off his coat, and work with the rest of the men . . . they developed new ideas in castings and soon the firm . . . became known throughout this section of the country for the excellence of their work."

"Along about 1887" (we intervene to remind the reader that the foundry is now twelve years old!), "Mr. Rentschler, who was still selling products of the firm, was in Dayton calling on an old customer. 'There's a new firm starting up down here,' said his friend. 'It's very small, has little money, but you might get some business there'".

"So Mr. Rentschler went down. He met a couple of young men in a shop (who) showed him some patterns. 'I'll take these', said Mr. Rentschler, 'and go down to Hamilton this afternoon and have castings up here by tomorrow.'"

"He kept his word, and from that moment, Mr. Rentschler and John H. Patterson, founder of the National Cash Register Co. of Dayton, were staunch personal friends and their business relations were always of the best."

"The Sohn & Rentschler Foundry made all of the castings for the NCR for 25 years or until the flood of 1913 took away their shop. Mr. Patterson had built a foundry himself but he would never consent to its existence so long as the Hamilton plant was able to provide him with his needs."[2] Adam had another casting firm untouched by the flood, The Hamilton Foundry & Machine Co.,[3] but it had numerous customers, whereas Sohn & Rentschler had been singularly dedicated to making parts just for NCR.

What a ride it had been for Adam: " . . . cash register sales, barely 1,000 in 1886, reached 15,000 in 1892 and 100,000 in 1910. The following year NCR sold its millionth machine. In 1884 there was no discernible demand, (but) by about 1910 (NCR) had made the cash register the essential tool of retailing, as necessary to the merchant as the block to the butcher or the anvil to the blacksmith."[4] He was victimized by the collapse of that new railroad bridge.

Not all of his business ventures succeeded. With Joseph B. Hughes, Adam in 1879 had started The Hamilton Tile Works to make floor and wall covering. It failed in 1897 and, though re-incorporated as Ohio Tile in 1901 with Henry Sohn as a partner, was dissolved for good in 1911. [5]

---

[2] Obituary, Hamilton Daily News, May 25, 1923.
[3] Gone bankrupt in 1985, Hamilton, then moved to Harrison, Ohio, was revived in 1986 by the author, but went under again in 1998.
[4] Mark Bernstein, Smithsonian Magazine, June, 1989
[5] pg. 113, Hamilton's Industrial Heritage, Richard Piland, Arcadia Publishing, 1915

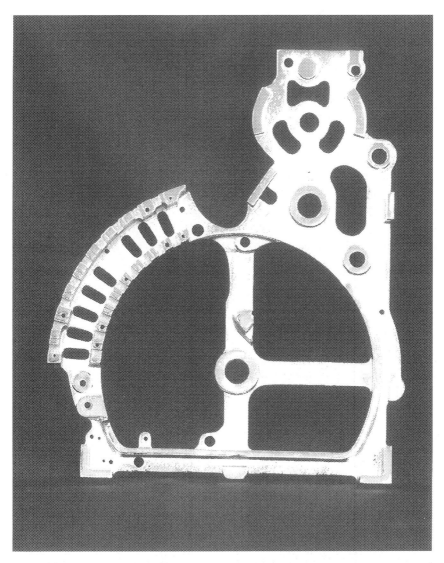

Sohn & Rentschler cast iron side frame for National Cash Register

CORLISS -- FOR A TIME, PEERLESS

In 1880, five years after the foundry was launched, Adam with two friends organized his second major buiness, called The Hooven, Owens, Rentschler Company (or "H.O.R.", less formally). The concern, which would become Adam's main legacy, was focused on building Corliss engines whose heyday lasted from around 1850 until 1920. Named for its New England inventor, George Henry Corliss, the concept tied together a natural gas engine and a steam engine, the high-temperature exhaust from the former fueling the latter, essentially anticipating its successor, the gas-turbine, in the 1920s [6]. Diesels would not appear until the 1890s.

To produce his engine, in the 1850s Corliss built a factory in Providence, Rhode Island, that ultimately employed 1,000 workers, and to protect his concept he amassed 60 patents. In 1867, competing against 100 of the best steam-engine makers in the world at the International Exposition in Paris, he won first prize. [7]

Unfortunately for Corliss, his basic patent expired in 1870. "Competitors leapt to copy his work, and their products

---

[6] "George Corliss' Engine Steamrolled Contenders," International Business Digest, pg. A3, 9/23/15
[7] Ibid

became known as Corliss engines." Nevertheless, with his own money, Corliss built an engine for the Centennial Exposition in Philadelphia in 1876. " . . . 10 million from all over the world came to see its 30,000 exhibits. The center of attention was Machinery Hall, which covered 13 acres.

"Powering all the Hall's devices was the world's largest steam engine, with a shaft 352 feet long and a flywheel weighing 56 tons, which operated almost silently. Corliss had paid the massive engine's $100,000 cost (equal to $2.3 million today) out of his own pocket." [8]

It is conceivable, however far-fetched, that Adam went to see the Exposition. It is a fact, though, that one of its attendees was a William Ford, who couldn't wait to relate what he saw to his 13 year-old son, Henry, when he got back home to their hard-scrabble farm in southern Michigan.[9] "(Henry) was already filled with enthusiasm for all things to do with steam."[10] In fact, his first job when he left the farm for the city would be in a steam-fired power plant belonging to Detroit Edison.

The significance of Henry Ford's interest in Corliss' technology will become clear later in this book.

---

[8] Ibid

[9] Henry Ford, The Wayward Capitalist, Carol Gildermas, pg 8, The Dial Press, 1981

[10] Henry Ford, Vincent Curcio, pg 7, Oxford University Press, 2013

5

THE MAIN CHANCE

Evidencing complete confidence in the growth potential of Corliss engines, Adam and his partners went about building their business with avengeance. They assembled a management team. Believers in vertical integration, they constructed nearly a dozen huge buildings, sprawling over some 30 acres north of downtown to accommodate the casting, forging and machining of steel and iron components. A few of these buildings were several hundred feet long and a hundred feet wide and fifty feet high to accommodate overhead cranes straddling the bays to move materiel. H.O.R. soon was employing several hundred workers.

Adam had managed to arrange outside financing (a $1 million loan, collateralized with the buildings) from a Cincinnati bank. It was also important that, in order to hog out their massive components, Niles Tool Works, builder of the largest milling machines in the world, was right next door, and that two major, north-south railroads straddled both sides of the complex to allow efficient flow of incoming raw material and outgoing finished product.

Photographs of H.O.R.'s factories at the end of the nineteenth century do not exist, but Adam's son-in-law, Sidney D. Waldon (Helen's husband), writing at the end of World War II when the successor company employed 4500 people (making a different type of engine), reported that "the present shop with

14

its very high bays was completed in 1902"[11], and an artist's rendering of the complex in 1945 appears towards the end of this book.

By 1900, H.O.R. had built over 700 Corliss engines and was the largest producer of them in the world. With 800 or so workers, it also was Hamilton's second largest employer, just behind Champion Coated Paper.

The 1913 flood did tremendous, though not irreparable, damage to H.O.R. In parts of the cavernous complex, the water was 40' high! Unlike the fate of Sohn & Rentschler, however, the Miami did not deliver a knock-out punch to H.O.R. – the physical plant was plain too massive. More importantly, the determination of Adam and his sons to persevere would prove too invincible.

---

[11] Sidney D. Waldon, "General Machinery Corporation, 1845-1945", William E. Rudge's Sons, Inc., New York, N.Y., 1945, pg.11

The New Factory Built 1902
The Largest Exclusive Corliss Engine Plant in the Country

PLANT OF
THE HOOVEN-OWENS-RENTSCHLER
HAMILTON, OHIO, U.S.A.

"With a view of producing along the lines of the highest efficiency and economy, the Hooven-Owens-Rentschler Company of Hamilton, Ohio, have within the last year reconstructed their entire plant and more than doubled it as to productive capacity". This work was commenced in January,1902, and the new building was completed in July of 1904

The scheme of arrangement of buildings, power plant, tracks, machines, etc., is that of Colonel J. C. Hooven, president of the company, and details were worked out by Mr. George Barkman, of Hamilton

Nothing was diminutative about H.O.R. Machinery
including this punch press (circa 1917)

"Lunch Time" at Caroliss Works of H.O.R.

6

A SECOND FAMILY

In 1883, his first two businesses under way, Adam, now 38, was married for a second time. His new bride, only 21, was Phoebe Schwab, from Hamilton. Her father, Peter, like his son-in-law, was a German immigrant and aspiring entrepreneur. He had founded the Cincinnati Brewing Company, whose beer had "met with such universal favor that . . . the company was incorporated with a capital of $250,000 in 1882,"[12]

The year they were married, Adam and Phoebe produced a son, Robert Peter . The next year (1884) they bought a 131-acre farm in Fairfield township, five miles east of Hamilton, and, in its modest, sandstone farm-house, they produced four more children: Gordon Sohn (1885), Frederick Brant (1887), Helen Dorothy (1890) and George Adam, Jr., or "Bud" (1892).

The time and toil of the buggy-rides to-and-from the city pretty soon trumped the peace and tranquility of the place in the country, however, and the family moved back to Hamilton in 1902 and sold the farm in 1906. (Gordon, though, then just finishing college, vowed he would someday buy back the farm!).

Further expanding his clutch of businesses, Adam at this time was constructing a 6-story structure downtown at the

---

[12] pg. 331, Concise History of Hamilton, Ohio, Stephen D. Conn, Volume II, 1901, Press of George Mitchell, Middletown, Ohio. The brewery would go bankrupt in 1919 with the onset of Prohibition.

corner of High and 2d Streets to house offices, including his own, and his two banks (Dime Savings and Citizens, run by Henry, the son from his first marriage). The Rentschler Building opened in 1906 and, aside from the Butler County Court House (across the street), would be Hamilton's tallest structure for 25 years.

The Rentschlers purchased a house at 643 Dayton Street, a commodious three-story Victorian mansion complete with stable. Their new home was on the far-east side of town, for Adam, half-an-hour to the office on foot, ten minutes by horse-and-buggy. Henry Sohn, Adam's first business partner, was next door. Adam and Phoebe would live there the rest of their lives.

Nominally Lutheran, the Rentschlers typically didn't go to church on Sundays. The author, in fact, does not recall his father, Bud, or aunt, Helen, ever going to church other than attending a wedding or a funeral. German wasn't spoken at home -- the author's father knew only a few words in German. Vacations, when taken, were ordinary, not extravagant. They would go by train to see Adam's oldest son, George, and his family in northern Indiana or to spend some time at French Lick, a resort some 50 miles northwest of Louisville. Adam never returned to Germany. Likely it never even crossed his mind.

Rentschler children and friends on steps of their home. – Fred (lower left), Gordon (upper left). Helen (upper right) and Bud (lower right). Circa 1895

7

THE HALLS OF IVY

Frugal in many respects, Adam and Phoebe believed that their children should receive as much formal education as possible. Encouraged by a minister (whose name is long forgotten), they sent their four sons after high school in Hamilton to Princeton University and their daughter, in lieu of local high school, to Ogontz, a preparatory school outside of Philadelphia.

The boys majored in liberal arts, except Fred who studied engineering. Robert was class of 1906; Gordon, 1907; Fred, 1909; and George, Jr., (Bud, as he was called), 1915. Robert, unfortunately had a nervous breakdown and was institutionalized his senior year.

His brothers' personalities, though, started to become manifest.

Gordon emerged as a leader. He was not only president of his senior class but chairman of the daily newspaper. He was so totally devoted to the school that he would become a life-time trustee of Princeton in 1920. Fred, shy by nature, evidently was absorbed by his classes and likely used free hours to hone his tennis skills. Bud simply had a good time. Paying the price for the fun he had as a senior rooming with F. Scott Fitzgerald (probably then starting to conceive in his head The Great Gatsby, that best-selling book in The

Twenties), Bud had to return for a fifth year in order to get his diploma.

After college, the three brothers came back to Hamilton, Gordon not to leave for good until age 40, Fred, 30, and Bud, almost 50. Remember, this was long before men routinely went to college, or, having graduated from college, went into the armed forces or graduate schools. Yet there were more fundamental realities at play here why they "came back to the nest".

First, there was so much work to do in their father's far-flung business empire – in fact, he'd just started up another company – to make cars! While during the summers they may have had jobs as "hourlies" in their family's shops, upon graduation, they joined management where their father needed them. Also, Adam was getting on in years – he'd turned 60 when Gordon graduated from Princeton. Significantly, they adored their parents and their parents them, and the siblings, each different, got along well enough with each other, snugly sequestered in their parents home at 643 Dayton Street. Finally, there was the lure of southern Ohio land – Gordon and Bud soon would each buy a farm there.

Some sense of the family's situation is revealed in a portion of a letter that Phoebe wrote her daughter, Helen, then a senior at Ogontz, a month or two after Gordon's graduation from Princeton: "Sohn & Rentschler are only working half a week. You know Papa is always much concerned about his people . . . and he takes it upon himself to help them keep the wolf from their doors. No doubt there will be much suffering among the working classes . . . the working man is afraid (of the banks) while in Papa he trusts. Gordon is looking fine. He has a new suit and overcoat. This morning, as he and Papa walked down the street, Jacob was sweeping the porch and I was watching from the screen door. Jacob said 'I bet our Gordon looks like a Senator; he is a fine looking fellow' . . . If our dear Robert was not as unfortunate all would be well. My dear Robert, God bless and care for him is my constant prayer . . . I almost forgot to tell you Papa lost his greatly prized umbrella . . . . He left it on the train."[13]

[13] Box 22, File 2, Mary C. Rentschler Collection, The New York Historical Society

Perhaps Adam's proudest physical structure was the Rentschler Building completed in 1906. Other than the Butler County Courthouse, it was Hamilton's tallest structure until 1929.

8

UNINTENDED CONSEQUENCES

When two years later, Fred returned to Hamilton from college, one might have thought that Adam would have assigned him to work alongside Gordon in one of his main businesses, H.O.R. or one of the two foundries, where the younger brother could be of real value. Instead, Adam had started up a brand-new concern to build automobiles, The Republic Motor Car Company, and put Fred in charge as "General Supervisor".

On the surface, this made no sense. Adam didn't need another business (he already had seven), and America didn't need another car company (it now had several hundred). Plus, their manufacture was starting to be rationalized, as manifest in Henry Ford who had begun to mass produce the Model T in 1907 and would assemble nearly 11,000 in 1910 alone.

Adam, evidently, felt that he needed to create some space between these two young men. Blessed with a strong mechanical aptitude, Fred was shy, if not retiring. Possessing enormous drive, his older brother tended to dominier. "Gordon," Fred would later write, "always tried to act ten or twenty years older than himself and I know took something of a fatherly interest in anything of importance, good or bad."[14]

An assembly operation, the Republic bought engines, radiators, fenders, etc., and put them together in its own building on the east side of Hamilton. Intriguingly, through his close friendship with John Patterson, Adam had gotten to know National Cash Register's chief engineers, Edward A. Deeds and Charles F. Kettering, who, "moonlighting" nights and weekends, had just invented the self-starter to replace the hand-crank on cars. These two gentlemen "spent many Sunday dinners at the Rentschler home (where) they planned and discussed the formation of The Republic Car Company," according to Fred's sister, Helen.[15]

Deeds and Kettering not only became shareholders in the new car company but also fitted the Republic with their self-starter. In so doing they became close friends of Fred, whom they invited to Dayton and introduced to their close friends, the Wright brothers, aviation's pioneers. And Fred was hooked! Surprising (maybe shocking) to his father, Fred would use his Republic car to drive to Dayton on weekends to pursue his love for airplanes. Aviation had dawned, and, in fact, it had dawned right there in Dayton, Ohio!

Incredible as it sounds, Fred at least once raced his Republic car against a plane piloted by Orville. Herewith a recapitulation many years later by Jim Blount, amateur historian and columnist for the Hamilton newspaper (it's a sure bet that Fred was the driver):

"A Hamilton-built automobile lost a highly-publicized race in 1910, but not to another car. The Republic's opponent . . . was an airplane piloted by one of the Wright brothers (who)

[14] Letter to Mary C. Rentschler, his sister-in-law, after Gordon's death. Folder 6, box 14, Mary C. Rentschler Collection, The New York Historical Society
[15] Report of "The Antique and Classic Car Club of Butler County," by John C. Slade, 6/23/11

in 1910 (had) started their highly-successful Wright Expedition Company with pilots they had trained at Huffman Prairie northeast of Dayton. They entertained crowds at fairs, carnivals, circuses and other events . . . Orville (the pilot that day) had reached an altitude of 2500 feet, reportedly, as high as ever he was up . . . (He) looked down on the 60-horsepower Republic going as fast as it could and kept about even with it until it was necessary to go ahead, then he let the wings of his air bird flap a little faster and he went by the Republic like a shot. Wright won by about a mile . . . as the whistles of the city blew and the thousands cheered."[16]

The Republic operation was shuttered in 1913. Though not affected directly by the Great Flood, the car company's financial performance never was robust because of the horde of competitors, and Adam needed his senior leaders to supervise the clean-up of HOR and gear up the sprawling complex for work he saw coming

Yet, while his father would growl that "aviation is a damn fool business, mostly for sportsmen,"[17] Fred had gotten captivated by flight and would be unhappy until he worked in the industry full-time.

---

[16] Article by Jim Blount, Hamilton Journal, August 7, 1996
[17] Jane C. Shipp, pamphlet, "Hartford Innovator", April 27, 2012

Briefly a builder of cars. Fred drives Republic (circa 1912)

9

APRES LES DELUGE

Proof positive of the wide-spread regard for the leadership skills of this 28 year-old, Gordon was named by the mayor of Hamilton as chairman of the Relief Committee within two hours of the collapse of the last bridge over the Great Miami River, March 25, 1913. The committee's purpose was to seek and coordinate outside aid coming into the city.[18] Once the waters receeded, the dead buried and the debris removed, the big question remained: how could Hamiltonians avoid another such calamity?

This conundrum pitted Ohioans against each other in a struggle of northerners and southerners not seen since the Civil War: the people closest to the Ohio River suffered the most, but the problem began with the people up-state. It would be a full five years before disagreements could be resolved and construction begun on a solution to the flooding.

Gordon and Ed Deeds, the Rentschler family's friend from Dayton, realized the solution had to be a comprehensive flood-control program for ALL of southwest Ohio, not a patch-work approach community-by-community. Deeds, by now, flush with money from selling his share of the self-starter business, was embarked on a 16-year sabbatical from National Cash Register.

---

[18] Jim Blount, Hamilton Journal, 10/6/93

Helping tame Ohio's great Miami River shaped Gordon's career.

Helping tame Ohio's great Miami River shaped Gordon's career.

Within weeks, Gordon and Deeds organized the Miami Conservation District, which quickly grew to nine members, one from each of the counties through which the river flowed. Proof of the seriousness of his intentions, Deeds, out of his own pocket, constructed a three-story office building in downtown Dayton to house the District's employees. Dogging the project, however, were law suits, including one that went all the way to the U.S. Supreme Court which did not finally rule in favor of the District until June 4, 1918.[19]

To head the project to tame the river, Deeds hired "the best flood control engineer in the United States," Arthur E. Morgan, who was selected two decades later to design the Tennessee Valley Authority (better known as the "TVA").

However, unlike the latter, this project was done completely with private funds, $35 million of 30-year bonds sold in 1919 through National City Bank's investment banking division, headed by Charles E. Mitchell, who took an immediate liking to Gordon, and shortly would reroute his career, as will be seen.

Finally approved and funded, the District widened the river, built levees and dams, and completed the project in April, 1923. To provide for payment of interest and amortization of principal on the District's bonds, property-owners in the nine affected counties would pay a modest tax for thirty years, or until 1949, when the debt was paid off in full.[20] The District, without question, proved a model agency of its kind in the history of the United States.

Not only would the Deeds' connection recast Gordon's business career but his social life, too. By now very good friends from working together on the District project, Deeds some time in 1921 or 1922 invited Gordon to lunch in Dayton

---

[19] Pgs. 161-162, Colonel Deeds, Industrial Builder, Isaac P. Marcosson, Dodd, Mead & Company, 1947

[20] Gordon would remain a director of the District until 1933 when his youngest brother, Bud, succeeded him

to help entertain Ted and Mary Atkins, a couple from Boston in their early thirties. Afterwards Gordon told Deeds how much Mary reminded him of his mother and how he'd like to marry such a nice person.[21] He would get his wish as, early in 1923, flying from Florida to Cuba, where his family had a sugar plantation, the Atkins crashed in the ocean, killing Ted and their two young sons. Mary and a girl with whom she was pregnant survived.[22] Four years later Gordon and Mary would get married.

---

[21] Interview with Phoebe R. Stanton, 1/29/16
[22] Pilot's account of crash, 1/13/23 (in possession of the author)

Gordon, probably in his early thirties (Circa 1915)

10

HIS LAST HURRAH!

Restored to working shape after the flood, H.O.R. would be blessed with orders and pushed to capacity in 1916, the year Adam turned 70. Gordon, though, by now was fully in control: "(he) is often in the works as in his office. Every one of the 1500 in his employ knows him personally. Hundreds call him unhesitatingly by his first name, for they have known him since boyhood."[23]

In August, although the United States had not yet entered World War I, Congress, concerned about the sinking of so many American ships carrying cargo to the Allies in Europe, created the "Emergency Fleet Corporation" to build boats to offset the losses to German submarines.

Astonishingly, looking back now, these ships, usually made of wood, were powered by steam engines, a forte of H.O.R., and Adam, the German immigrant, threw himself wholeheartedly behind the cause, vowing to become "the largest builder of marine engines in the world." Gordon, returning from "The Marine General Conference" in Washington, D.C., boasted "I told these Washington folks we were going to build more marine engines and better marine engines than anybody

---

[23] A History of Hooven, Owens, Rentschler, Box 14, Mary C. Rentschler Collection, New York Historical Society

else," and, as a result, H.O.R. started building steam engines at a rate of one per day for the Emergency Fleet Corporation."[24]

However, something far more amazing than building these marine engines was going on at H.O.R. in 1916: the Rentschlers were completing the construction of nine humongous-size Corliss engine-generators to provide electricity for Henry Ford's first plant in Highland Park (four miles northwest of downtown Detroit) where the Model T was being assembled.

Ford, shrewdly only committing capital in his first factory as the popularity of his car grew, had installed the world's first moving assembly line in 1913, when he would build 185,000 vehicles, or half of the cars made in America. He was now ready to produce his own electricity rather than buy power from Detroit Edison (his first employer, it will be recalled!).[25]

At a price of around $1 million, the Rentschlers supplied nine Corliss-driven engine-generators for the power plant, which was housed in its own building, approximately 400' long by 200' wide, or roughly the size of the inside of a professional football stadium. Each engine produced 6,000 horsepower and drove a 4,000 kilowatt DC generator. The combination engine-generator weighed 750 tons and was 82' long by 46' wide, and, its major pieces disassembled, was transported by railroad from the Hamilton factory to the Michigan site on 5 flat cars -- 45 flat cars in total![26]

Henry Ford, himself, reportedly was delighted with the results. After the closure of Highland Park in 1927 (it had produced half of the cars made in America to that point), one of the H.O.R. engine-generators was sent to the Henry Ford

---

[24] The Louisiana Planter and Sugar Manufacturer, 12/27/23, Lane Library, Hamilton, Ohio

[25] Steve Watts, The People's Tycoon, Alfred A. Knopf, 2015, pgs. 137-139

[26] Jim Blount, "Hamilton's Engines Powered Ford's Highland Park Plant," Hamilton Journal News, A9, 8/3/05

Museum in Dearborn, MI where it still sets with a sign that says: "These engines represented for Mr. Ford the pinnacle of power, efficiency and beauty."[27] It would be Adam's "last hurrah".

[27] The People's Tycoon, pg. 138

H.O.R (circa 1912 – 1915) built nine Corliss engines to provide electricity for Ford's Highland Park factory which made Model Ts.

On display at Henry Ford Museum. Dearborn, MI is a Corliss engine built by Hooven Owens Rentschler. Diameter of the flywheel is 15 feet.

A Large Finished Fly Wheel For
A Hamilton Corliss Engine

AOR
354

We believe this this may be one of the large flywheels for Henry Ford's, Highland Park power plant SteamGas engines. It was pored into a mold and machined to final dimensions as shown in previous slide in HOR's Hamilton foundry and machine shops

The Video shows Henry Ford taking visitors through the Highland Park Mi. model T assembly plant, power plant and shows the completed fly wheel in operation on a Hamilton engine

Henry Ford with his Model T

11

TENDING THE HOME FIRES

Never discharged from the institution where he was sent from Princeton with that unknown ailment, Bob, the oldest son of Adam and Phoebe, died in 1915, age 32. So close to her first-born (as we have recounted) mother Phoebe passed away a year later, 1916, quite possibly of a "broken heart". She was only 55 but had been married to Adam 34 years.

Astonishingly (to us in our era, anyway), at that point in time the other four children of his second marriage, all single, still lived at home with Adam, now 71: Gordon, age 31; Fred, 29; Helen, 26; and Bud, 24. Helen oversaw the house-keeping at 643 Dayton Street where there was live-in help (a cook and a maid) and a yard-man.

With all hands needed to produce the gargantuan order from Ford for the Corliss engine-generators, the three young men worked at H.O.R. until America entered World War I in 1917. Then, Fred and Bud became officers in The Signal Corps (predecessor of the Army air force). Gordon remained in Hamilton as a civilian – he had poor eye-sight and had replaced his father as president of H.O.R. and The Hamilton Foundry & Machine Co., the family's two main businesses.

Fred would never work in Hamilton again, as we shall see. In 1921, however, he married a Hamilton lady, Faye Belden, the daughter of an overhead-crane operator at H.O.R. Bud, though, came back at war's end to help Gordon find new business for H.O.R., staggered when the Navy cancelled the remaining orders for steam engines on Armistice Day. With the Corliss engine business seen sliding into obsolescence within a decade, one of Bud's main assignments was to make and sell diesel engines under license from a German firm, Maschinenfabrik Augsburg Nuremberg (or "M.A.N.")

Gordon, on top of his general management duties, personally assumed responsibility for a civilian business that suddenly boomed: a line of equipment to process Cuban sugar-cane, including (ironically) a Corliss-powered milling machine that burned stalks for fuel. The Great War had vastly stimulated the cane industry because, with the traditional source of supply --the sugar-beet farms of northern France -- turned into brutal battle fields, the world was suddenly dependent on Cuba for its sweeteners.

Not surprisingly, prices had sky-rocketed, from a low of 2 cents per pound in 1914 to a high of 22 cents in early 1920, encouraging growers to invest heavily in modernizing and expanding their plantations in Cuba. However, with the war ended and beet production begun again in Europe, sugar prices reverted back to 2 cents by 1921-1922.[28]

Initially profitable for H.O.R., but ultimately problematic, the Cuban sugar business would play a crucial role in Gordon's career. To try to collect money, he would visit Cuba frequently over the next few years, sometimes accompanied by Edward Deeds, who'd become a close friend from their work at the Miami Conservancy District (made a Colonel during the war, as we shall see) and they would get to know executives from National City Bank, which had lent huge sums of money to the growers. These connections would ultimately set Gordon on a fresh career path that pulled him out of Hamilton – but not until after his father had died.

---

[28] pg. 357, Colonel Deeds, Industrial Builder, Isaac F. Marcosson, Dodd, Mead & Co., 1947

Adam's "Other" Main Business: The Hamilton Foundry & Machine CO. as seen in 1953

12

STARTING TO TAXI
. . . SLOWLY

Given his work at H.O.R. had taught him something about manufacturing and his "fling at making autos . . . about engines"[29], it is no surprise that Fred, commissioned a Captain, was assigned as head inspector of production at the newly-formed Wright-Martin Company's factories in Long Island and New Jersey, which, under license by the French government, made Hispano-Suiza (or "Hisso") aircraft that boasted "one of the best engines of World War I,"[30] -- of course, water-cooled, like automobile motors.

Ironically, Fred missed out on far-and-away America's greatest contribution to the Allied air campaign: the Liberty engine program that, in one year's time, produced 24,475 12-cylinder, water-cooled, essentially automobile motors cobbled together by the leading car-builders under the leadership of Fred's friend from Dayton, Edward A. Deeds, accordingly appointed the rank of Colonel by President Woodrow Wilson.

At war's end, November 1918, Wright-Martin was liquidated, but not before its directors "put aside $3 million to form a small

---

[29] Cover story on Fred, "Mr. Horsepower" Time magazine, May 28, 1951
[30] Page 10, The Engines of Pratt & Whitney; A Technical History, Jack Connors, American Institute of Aeronautics and Astronautics, 2010

aviation company," called Wright Aeronautical, focused solely on engines, located in the New Jersey plant and led by Fred. Bankrolled by a huge sum of money for that time, he'd formed a small but evidently strong management team, including a young engineer with a degree from Massachusetts Institute of Technology, George J. Mead.

Coming out of the hostilities, America's aviation industry was a mess, not only due to the huge inventory over-hang of Liberty engines -- only 1,100 or so ever saw combat in Europe, the balance mangled in plane-crashes, converted to carry U.S. mail, adapted for civilian uses or scrapped --but also because of the confusion about what the future held for airplanes and what type of engines would power them -- water or air-cooled? The main business of Wright, the most successful aviation firm in America, incredible as it seems, was producing each month a few water-cooled "Hissos" for the U.S. military.

The agent-for-change in this melodrama was, intriguingly, the U.S. Navy. The Washington Conference, held by America and its European allies, had banned construction of battleships for the time being. Accordingly, the Navy set its sights on building what is now called an aircraft carrier (with tiny reconnaissance planes for spotting enemy ships). However short of funds (with money unavailable after the war), the Navy in 1921 converted the USS Langley (a worn-out collier that had hauled coal to ships-of-the-line) into a crude "flat top" by fabricating over its hull a deck for take-off and landing and installing in its hold a freight elevator for storing its planes (which, of course, dictated they be tiny).

To power aircraft for the Langley, the Navy turned to arguably the most innovative person in the industry at the time, Charles L. Lawrance, a Yale graduate four years older than Fred, who, at the start of the Great War, using a French design, had built America's first air-cooled aircraft engine in a "completely inadequate" three-story loft in Manhattan (lacking money for machine tools, for example, Lawrance had to buy finished parts).[31]

A "plugger", Lawrance, had introduced a 65 horsepower model (the L) in 1919, a 147 horsepower version (the R) in 1920, and, then, in 1921, a 200 horsepower power-plant (the J-1). The motor weighed just 476 pounds, and "passed muster" with the Navy which commanded that the J-1 be fitted on every flivver assigned the Langley.[32]

But the Navy was not done with Fred!

[31] For complete disclosure, he is the great grandfather of my son-in-law, Peter Webel

[32] Pgs. 169-170, The Origins of the Air-Cooled Engine in the United States; Development of the Aircraft Engine, Robert Schlaifer, Harvard University, Boston MA, 1950

13

STEPPING OUT

Possibly signaling an interest to spend the rest of his life in Hamilton, Gordon, good to his word as a small boy, in 1917 repurchased his birthplace, the 131-acre homestead his father had sold when they moved to town in 1893. And between 1919 and 1924 he bought another 212 contiguous acres, for a total of 343, creating a very large farm at a time when field work was still predominantly done with horses and mules. As long as he resided in Hamilton, however, Gordon would live in his father's house.

Bud, after his return from the military in 1918, bought a home with a few acres, just south of the city limits, where he raised Doberman Pinschers, and, on his 30th birthday in 1922 he married Bessie Joan Morrison, an event that likely caused lots of gossip in Hamilton.

Orphaned at birth in Lima, Ohio, Joan (as she became known) had been raised by adoptive parents in nearby Upper Sandusky, Ohio. Through her own perseverance, evidently, she became an "extremely famous" dancer in New York City during the "Nineteen Teens", sometimes paired with Rudolph Valentino[33]. Bud, who loved to dance, probably met her at a cabaret on a business trip.

By all accounts well-paid, she used her money to fund events "doing men's stuff" to boost the status of ladies – a

---

[33] per Ms. Barb Nicolls, New Castle PA, an authority on Rudolph Valentino

"womens 'libber'", she'd be called today. As example, the summer of 1915 she organized a cross-country automobile-trip in two seven-passenger Paige-Detroit sedans (all expenses paid by their manufacturer), driving the lead car herself, with a lady friend, while a chauffeur and a maid rode in the back-up car, advancing the notion of women's equality with men.[34] In another event to draw attention, she charted a sea-pane to fly the length of Manhattan over the Hudson River to "tender the greetings of the theatrical profession to 'the illustrious warrior", General John J. Pershing, returning to the U.S. on an ocean liner," September 8, 1919.[35]

Joan's dancing career abruptly ended January, 1920, with the passage of the Eighteenth Amendment that, prohibiting the use of liquor, closed saloons across America. At that point, Bud, with his important job, handsome looks, and small farm with a pack of Dobermans must have seemed like a good deal, and, presuming they loved each other, their marriage followed.

Bud and Joan would have no children -- likely because she was already in her late thirties on their wedding day. How long they lived together is not known (though they were listed as guests on the program handed out at the dedication of Rentschler Field in Hartford, 1931).

A worrisome letter, though, from Gordon to Helen in the summer of 1927 casts a disturbing light on his youngest brother: "I don't get Bud's drift . . . I have always loved Bud just like he were my son – more than a brother. I have always considered him by best friend . . . He went away. . . this is not the real Bud. This is a Bud under a strange spell . . . Bud is remaking his own life. Maybe the happiness he brings to some will compensate for the ache he brings to others. My own conscience tells me

---

[34] Variety, June 18, 1915
[35] New York's "The Evening Telegraph", pg.1, September 8, 1919

he is wrong."[36] Gordon perhaps was alluding to Bud spending too much time away from the job of running the family's main business.

After fourteen years of marriage (but the last several years likely living apart), Bud and Joan officially got divorced on September 21, 1936 in Newport, Kentucky, across the Ohio River from Cincinnati. Two months later he married Rita R. Mitchell, only daughter of Gordon's one-time boss and mother of the author and his two brothers, George A. Jr. and Frederick B. II.

---

[36] Box 22, File 9, Mary C. Rentschler Collection, The New York Historical Society

14

PASSING OF THE TORCH

Adam generally was in fair health and good spirits the last few years of his life. Representative of his mind-set is a letter to Helen (visiting in Maine the summer before his death) where he wrote: "Everything is going along nicely. I am feeling about the same as I did when you left. The house is very lonesome without you. Gordon hasn't come back yet, and Bud is away most of the time. I hope you will enjoy every minute of your stay there, in as short a time as you can. You can't come home any too soon."[37]

Adam died at his home, May 23, 1923, six weeks short of his 77h birthday. Five of his six surviving children attended the funeral at 643 Dayton Avenue (note, not in a church) and the burial at near-by Greenwood Cemetery next to his second wife, Phoebe. Bud was in Copenhagen on a sales trip.

In a cover story on son Fred years later, Time magazine wrote about his father: "Orphaned at eleven, Adam had to scratch hard for every penny, scratched so hard that he eventually became a millionaire out of the foundry he started in Hamilton, Ohio. 'Only two things are worth having', Adam always said, 'money in the bank and pig iron in the mold.'"[38]

---

[37] Box 22, File 2, Mary C. Rentschler Collection, The New York Historical Society

[38] "Mr. Horsepower", cover story, Time magazine, May 28, 1951

One of the two local newspapers opined in its obituary that the Rentschler Building was only "an incidental monument" to Adam's success – "the real physical monuments to Mr. Rentschler are the industrial plants and buildings of which he was the main inspiration. These . . . are giving employment to thousands of people . . . "[39]

His children had to have been deeply respectful of, if not reverential to, their father – what he had done for his family, his city and his nation; what he had signified, in terms of honesty, charity, patriotism and hard work; how he had loved their mother; and what wealth he had amassed.

Probated the next year, Adam's will totaled $1,886,000, or $314,000 for each of his six surviving children:

Will of George Adam Rentschler[40]

Stocks:	
The Hooven, Owens, Rentschler Co.	$569,000
The Hamilton Foundry & Machine Co.	325,000
G. A. Rentschler Co.	219,000
Citizens Bank/Dime Savings	111,000
Other:	662,000
Total:	$1,886,000

It would be difficult to estimate the worth of Adam's will in today's dollars (a clue may lie in that it included a new Lincoln Victoria automobile purchased for $2,300). In truth, his assets were pretty illiquid. He had escrowed about 20% ($350,000) for maintenance and/or expansion of The Rentschler Building. More significantly, two-thirds of his wealth was bound up in closely-held stocks that would only be sold at some significant discount.

---

[39] Hamilton Evening Journal, May 25, 1923
[40] in possession of the author

An incredible accomplishment for a poor, orphaned immigrant. Yet whatever wealth they were left would not alter the careers of Gordon, Fred and Bud. Significantly, however, Gordon and Fred were no longer in his orbit. As long as their father lived, neither would take the big first step that defined his career – Gordon accepting a seat on the board of National City Bank and Fred leaving Wright to form his own firm.

Rentschler brother's sister Helen, who married Sidney D. Waldon, executive with Packard and Cadillac in their early years

15

ONE TOUGH YANKEE

The biography of Charles Edwin Mitchell is not the "rags-to-riches" type of George Adam Rentschler, yet pretty close. He was born in 1877 (seven years before Gordon) in Chelsea, Massachusetts, a blue-collar town just north of Boston (fittingly, home of Horatio Alger which became America's all-time, best-selling novelist with his books on "How to Succeed"). Serving a term or two as mayor, his father ran a wholesale grocery business that went broke in Charlie's junior year at Amherst, requiring him to work the rest of the way to pay his board and tuition.[41]

He started out his career in 1899 with Western Electric in Chicago, where he met his future wife, Elizabeth Rend, daughter of a modestly successful operator of a southern Illinois coal mine. Charlie moved back East in 1907 to work for the Trust Company of New York as a bond salesman at which he excelled. Emboldened by his success, he soon set up his own firm to sell bonds, but, word of his ability spreading, was recruited in 1916 to run the investment banking division of National City Bank, one of the larger banks in New York.

". . . his timing was excellent; he assumed the helm of the securities affiliate just before the sale of Liberty bonds during World War I primed the burgeoning middle class to buy

---

[41] Pg. 75, The Hellhound of Wall Street, Michael Perino, The Penguin Press, 2010

securities. Within a few years, the National City Company had 1400 employees with branches across the country and around the globe."[42] In four years Mitchell had built the business into "the largest distributor of securities in the United States."[43] He was on the cusp, though, of much bigger accomplishment.

The parent company had wagered that good times would last forever for the Cuban sugar industry. And it had acted accordingly. "In 1919 alone, the bank opened twenty-two branches in Cuba" and soon "held nearly 20 percent of the loans outstanding in the Cuban banking system (or) an astounding 80 percent of its total capital . . ."[44]. But in November, 1920, the price of sugar tumbled to just a penny per pound when, as related earlier, those European growers got back into the business, and, more broadly, the U.S. ran into a recession. Reflecting this turmoil, the bank churned through three presidents in just three years.

As a result, given his phenomenal performance heading the investment banking division, the directors of National City in May, 1921 selected Mitchell, just 43 years old, to run the largest commercial bank in the United States, although he had never worked in a commercial bank a single day of his life.

Since the company's foremost problem was Cuba, Mitchell's first step was to conduct a thorough investigation of the sugar business, and, in this regard, to survey the bank's properties he quickly enlisted the help of Gordon Rentschler (whom, as seen, he'd met a couple of years earlier as underwriter for the bonds of the Miami Conservancy District). Given the gravity of the request, Gordon, with Colonel Deeds at his side, left Ohio for Cuba within a couple of weeks.

---

[42] Ibid, pg.78

[43] Pg. 107, Citibank, 1812-1970, Harold V. Cleveland and Thomas F. Huertas, Harvard University Press, 1985

[44] Pg. 79, Perino

16

WAFTED BY SEA BREEZES

Broke but ambitious, the U. S. Navy after World War I had the vision in the early 'Twenties that carrier-based airplanes might have use well beyond reconnaissance – they could be fitted with guns and bombs and deployed to attack enemy ships and aircraft. Presciently came an announcement that the Navy, in fact, was laying the keel for REAL "flat-tops" -- the Saratoga and the Lexington -- with launch dates in 1925.

Accordingly, as Lawrance's little company began producing the J-1, the Navy asked for bids for larger engines from its two established suppliers, Curtiss Aircraft and Wright Aeronautical. Incredibly, from today's perspective, neither would tender an offer! Curtiss was "completely uninterested" and Wright explained that, in terms of air-cooled technology, it was focused only on larger motors.[45]

Not surprisingly, the admirals took umbrage. The Navy fired back at Rentschler that it would not only NOT buy any more water-cooled "Hissos" but would also cannibalize parts from its existing fleet rather than order any more spares (which logically provided the bulk of Wright's profits).

Further, the Navy told Fred that his shortest route to producing a 200 horse-power air-cooled engine was to purchase Lawrance Aero-Engine Corporation and told Charles

---

[45] pg. 174. Development of the Aircraft Engine in the United States, Robert Schlaifer, Harvard U. Boston MA, 1950

Lawrance that, even though his company was making money, "it would be advantageous to sell out to Wright and thus put the future development as well as the production of the J-1 in the hands of a company with much greater resources."[46]

Wright purchased Lawrance Aero-Engine for $500,000 on May 15, 1923, a week before Fred's father died. Ironically, Fred had bought his way in to the U.S.'s best air-cooled engine technology of the day, and was forced to do so, at that. The acquisition of Lawrance's business made Wright America's biggest airplane-engine manufacturer and maybe its best – four years later, a J-5, descendant of the J-1, would power Charles Lindbergh's Spirit of St. Louis non-stop across the Atlantic in 33 hours. Fred, however, was set to quit Wright Aeronautical.

---

[46] Ibid. Wright made Lawrance a vice-president.

17

THE SOUTHERN
TEMPTRESS

"Apart from the depressed price of sugar, the big problem (that National City faced in Cuba) was that $25 million in loans depended on sugar properties (plantations and mills) that had not been ready to produce when sugar prices collapsed in 1921, forcing their owners into default . . . In their uncompleted state, the market value of the mills and plantations, which the bank had acquired through foreclosure, was practically nil."[47]

Returning from Cuba in late 1922, Colonel Deeds and Gordon (who, as seen, himself was trying to collect money owed H.O.R.) reported that "with some additional investment, the properties could repay the bank and yield a decent return." Mitchell, joining them in Cuba the following January, agreed with their findings and decided that "the bank should go into the sugar business in a big way and bet on the recovery of sugar to a higher price. To oversee the operation, the directors hired Rentschler and Deeds, who formed a firm called General Sugar Corporation to manage the properties . . . Within a year, the unfinished plantations, mills and railroads were producing sugar.

---

[47] pg. 108, Citibank, 1812-1970, Harold Cleveland and Thomas Huertas, Harvard University Press, 1985

"When the price of sugar recovered to five cents a pound in 1923, the Rentschler-Deeds report was confirmed. The bank's sugar business began to run in the black. . . . In October of that year Rentschler joined the bank's board of directors with responsibility for overseeing (its) sugar interests.

However, "ultimately, the bank would pay dearly for its continued exposure to sugar . . . the price of Cuban sugar never made a lasting comeback . . . Rentschler's and Deed's recommendations had been technically but not economically sound, for they had not correctly anticipated developments in the world's sugar market. The price fell in 1925 and did not exceed four cents a pound again until World War II. After 1926 even General Sugar's modernized mills operated in the red."[48]

Mitchell, though, decided NOT to write off the Cuban loans, since "keeping the Cuban credits on the books . . . preserved the bank's capital (which) enabled him to take advantage of the era of growth and prosperity that lay just ahead. Had he followed a more conservative course, writing off the $25 million in loans on uncompleted projects immediately, the cutback in the bank's capital funds would have forced him to set more modest goals for expansion. The Cuban decision allowed him to adopt a forward-looking strategy not only at home but abroad. In the course of the 1920s the expansion of the bank's capital and portfolio was so rapid that the sugar loans gradually receded from view."[49]

It is to Mitchell's credit that, right at the outset of his presidency, he immersed himself in the sugar industry to gain a full understanding of the business. If he decided to retain the bank's position (which he did), he would know how to keep things under control.

---

[48] pg. 109
[49] pg. 110

Great Sugar Mill is Being Completed Here

The Republic News, Hamilton, Ohio
1916

One of many cane sugar mills in Cuba, built by The Hooven, Owens, Rentschler Co.

It consists of one 23 roll installation consisting of one 42" x 87" Two Roll Crusher and one 36" x 84" crusher

The video above shows the completed mill in operation driven by a Hamilton Corliss steam engine

18

FLYING THROUGH
THE CLOUDS

As the 'twenties unfolded, it was not apparent what was eating at Fred, piloting Wright Aeronautical.

He later would recall that, before the war, there existed "the national myth that . . . within a few months U. S. planes would darken the skies over Europe . . . but now, in 1924, six years after The Armistice, "we were still adrift without an aviation policy, indisputably a third-rate air power, well behind both Great Britain and France."[50]

Nevertheless, he would explain, "Wright was a going, vigorous factor in the power-plant field . . . it was the only company which consistently was earning reasonable profits and continuing to expand its horizon and business."[51]

However, Fred had to be told by the Navy to put his company's emphasis on air-cooled, rather than water-cooled, engines, and, along these lines, to buy Lawrance's firm.

Yet, interestingly, Fred's problem ultimately was not the environment surrounding the aircraft engine business. The issue was internal.

---

[50] pg. 29, The Pratt & Whitney Story, Pratt & Whitney division of United Aircraft Company, August, 1950

[51] pg. 10, The Engines of Pratt & Whitney; A Technical History, Jack Connors, American Institute of Aeronautics and Astronautics, 2010

Fred would relate: "I personally was not at all satisfied in my position at Wright, and all of this dissatisfaction had to do with those above me, our Board of Directors . . . almost all investment bankers . . . none of whom was a substantial shareholder . . . (or) took any real interest in (the company's) affairs or its management.

"Finally, it reached a point where I was discouraged enough to feel that I should give it up and return to Hamilton . . . following the death of my father" in May, 1923.[52]

"However, an illness prevented any immediate action, except for my resignation from Wright . . . in June or July of 1924. (But) toward the first of the year, I had completely recovered and . . . found it virtually impossible to give up the thought of not going on with aviation . . . what had become a consuming passion."[53]

---

[52] Ibid, pg. 12. The birth of their first child, Helen, that summer might have lent strength to the urge to go home to Hamilton.
[53] Ibid.

Wasp-Powered Corsairs cover deck of Navy Carrier, Saratoga. This is the very same ship, sunk by the Japanese in World War II, that was found early in 2018 two miles below the surface and 500 miles off the east coast of Australia.

The U.S. Navy took nearly all of Pratt & Whitney's first year production to equip its first carriers with Vought Corsairs

19

THE BROTHERS THREE

Their ultimate careers not manifest until after the death of their father in 1923, how alike were Gordon, Fred and Bud is the subject of this chapter. How different were they is described later in the book[54]

- they had tremendous admiration and affection for their father, mother, sister, and each other
- they believed in hard work
- they stayed close
- they were married to the same women for over thirty years (in Bud's case, his second wife)
- they adored their children (each had three)
- they were prejudiced against Jews and people of color, in general terms, but respectful, one-on-one
- they smoked cigarettes copiously, though Bud switched to a pipe eventually
- they drank alcohol fairly heavily and consistently -- usually 2 cocktails before dinner each night
- they believed in God but generally avoided Sunday church services (Fred attending "when in the mood")
- they were ardent Republicans -- all three despised President Franklin Delano Roosevelt – who, as we shall

---

[54] certain "anecdotes" of Gordon supplied by his daughter, Phoebe Rentschler Stanton, and of Fred, by his son-in-law, William Cassidy

see, threw huge roadblocks in front of the careers of Gordon and Fred

Gordon openly backed Wendell Willkie in the 1940 election). Bud fervently supported Robert A. Taft in the 1948 and 1952 GOP primaries

- Gordon and Bud each belonged to 6-8 outside Boards of Directors (Fred limited himself to just the Hartford Hospital, due to time constraints)
- they were athletic (tennis, Bud and Fred -- the latter played nearly every day; Gordon, golf, his eyes not good for tennis)
- they never learned a foreign language
- they made, and spent, lots of money
- they threw themselves behind the Allied cause in World War I and II, despite their German lineage
- they belonged to The Links, a men's club in New York City

THE POLITICIAN

In making him an officer of National City, Mitchell evidently perceived in Gordon, seven years his junior, the same things seen by classmates at Princeton, workers in the family's businesses in Hamilton, and now employees of the bank: a "born leader".

Writing in late 1925 a few months after Gordon had accepted the position, a columnist for the New York World wrote:

"Rentschler is about six feet tall, and weighs around 185 pounds. There is a slight stoop to the thick shoulders and a forward thrust of the neck. His brown hair is close-cropped and parted in the middle. Blue eyes peer alertly thought thick-lensed spectacles. The nose is large enough to be called aggressive. His chin appears small because of the fleshy throat, but juts out to a firm point.

"In business hours his conversation is economical and orderly to an almost mathematical degree . . . (his) voice is deep and yet faintly nasal. It carries the easy assurance most successful men display. Above all, it is a friendly voice.

"The composite impression is one of boyish directness, unaffected and avid interest in the people and things around him. He is a man most persons would like on brief acquaintance . . .

"It is obvious the bank is a hobby with him. He gets a tremendous kick out of it. His next greatest interest is Princeton University, of which he is a charter trustee.

"'I went to Princeton as a country boy,'" he explained gravely, "'and I got a great deal out of it. It was an opportunity to see how other people lived, to learn what they did and what they thought. Oh, I'm only repaying some of the obligations I feel.'"[55]

Five years later, upon Gordon's promotion to the presidency of National City Bank, Fortune magazine (just two years old) wrote about him: "There is evident an almost limitless resistance to nervous strain. With energy to spare (he) talks volubly and convincingly . . . He is at least as much at ease with the Hamilton mechanics as with his Locust Valley neighbors . . . he would have made a first-rate politician."[56]

An appealing aspect of him, Gordon was grounded, quite literally, by soil, that is, the family farm he had reconstituted following World War I. Visiting his home-town on business in 1937, he wrote Mary, his wife: "It was pleasant to be in Hamilton . . . 'The Farm' looks very well . . . the boys (John Smith, the farmer, and a helper) have everything in 'apple pie' order (particularly gratifying because they did not know I was coming) . . . the pasture fields have never been more lush and, of course, all of the live-stock show the plain results of it."[57]

Again, in a letter in 1940 to his sister, Helen, and her husband, Sidney Waldon, about moving to "The Farm" from Michigan so he could help Bud manage the frenzied work-load at General Machinery: " . . . I always felt so keenly a love of the old place and all it stands for which will give them an understanding of the soil and the sense of security that comes from it . . . and the feeling that their roots belong somewhere that has meant so much to both of us."[58]

---

[55] Lawrence Stern, New York World, December 10, 1925

[56] "Scenario of Two Young Men," Fortune, November, 1930, pgs. 73-76, no by-line, presumably written by the editors.

[57] File 4, Box 10, Mary C. Rentschler Collection, The New York Historical Society

[58] File 12, Box 22, Mary C. Rentschler Collection, The New York Historical Society

THE MECHANIC

Like his father, Fred was an entrepreneur. Unlike his father (and his two brothers), though, Fred was "a man of few words" – or maybe, more exactly, engrossed with thoughts of aircraft engines.

"Fred is a different matter" than Gordon, wrote Fortune in its November 1930 issue. "Fred is the mechanic as executive. He has the interests, the patience, the sense of precision and of detail, the unworldliness of the expert mechanic. He has none of Gordon's friendliness and eloquent speech. He is shy and reserved with people and only unguarded with machines . . . He would rather make motors than money."[59]

In its cover story on him 21 years later, Time magazine described Fred as "one who thought, talked, breathed and dreamt engines. His tall (6'2"), lithe-muscled figure is as straight as a master rod, and, his face, as emotionless as a cylinder head." The publication noted "Rentschler was a private man who used memos to notify top people of raises rather than direct contact – even those who knew him for more than 20 years called him 'Mr. Rentschler'."[60]

In fact, even though Fred was an accomplished pilot (borrowing the company's Chance Vought Corsair), he didn't

---

[59] Fortune, November, 1930, pg. 76 (no by-line assigned).
[60] Time, May 28, 1951, pg. 30

have much time for recreational flying -- he was way too engrossed in solving technical problems.

An anecdote explains some of the difference between Gordon and Fred. When he moved to New York City from Hamilton, Gordon hired as his private secretary a diminutive (maybe 5' tall) gentleman, named Stewart Mapes. Gordon, however, "ran him ragged" and admitted it. He told Mapes that his brother Fred would be a much nicer boss, and, after he went and had an interview, Mapes was offered a position and worked for Fred until his retirement.[61]

That in Hartford he would live in a huge mansion and be chauffeured in a Rolls Royce was likely on account of his wife, Faye. That in retirement he would live in Florida in the former guest house of a resort hotel clearly seems to have been his idea

A mark of the introvert, Fred sadly kept a lot of things inside himself, the most notable example, as we shall see, his unforgiving view of the Roosevelt administration for breaking up the business that he and Bill Boeing would create.

---

[61] Anecdote furnished by Howard Wright, Renbrook School administrator, Hartford CT

Fred Rentschler on the front steps of the Pratt
& Whitney office in Hartford, circa 1928

THE SALESMAN

The author never got the idea that his father, Bud, starting in 1925, enjoyed running H.O.R., which became General Machinery, then Lima-Hamilton, then Baldwin-Lima-Hamilton, that was merged into Armour & Co. in 1965, over a stretch of 40 years. Ironically, by contrast, Fred was CEO (chief executive officer) of his aircraft-engine firm for 27 years (1926-1953) and Gordon was CEO of Citibank just 8 years (1940-1948).

That he was seen as a competent executive, though, is shown in the boards of directors he served living in Ohio -- Fifth Third Union Bank, Powell Valve, Philip Carey (roofing material), and Cincinnati Bell Telephone, and later (after taking over Baldwin Locomotive) living in New York -- Armour & Co., Barber Oil, and U.S. Lines. And he took these board memberships seriously (the author remembers one hot August day of 1963 him returning from an Armour board meeting in disbelief because, he related, "they say they're losing money on every hog they slaughter, yet they claim the answer is to run more animals through."!

Managing "the family business", especially (as we shall see) twenty years making diesel-electric locomotives in head-to-head competition with both General Motors and General Electric, was not a job for the timid. The author remembers, too well, a summer evening in 1963 at the Chicago Club being introduced to Benjamin F. Biaggini, then chairman of the

Southern Pacific Railroad, who stated bluntly: "Your father sold me a lot of engines that didn't work."!

In the "Thirties", two things arrived in Hamilton that my father loathed but was helpless to combat: unionization that emanated from Detroit and "hillbillies" that emigrated from southeastern Kentucky. He wouldn't miss either one when he moved East.

He was devoted to his family. He'd tell his young boys to "stick together" and, for illustration, take wooden matches and show us how much easier it was to break one compared to three. My mother and he settled on a family motto she had inscribed on a gold ring in Latin: "nostros coramos," which they translated as "we look after our own". Usually leaving home by train on business trips Sunday night, "Pop" generally managed to get back Thursday for supper which, unfailingly, was pork-chops, baked beans and lemon pie.

In a general sense (in keeping with the times and probably his brothers), Bud was prejudiced against Jews and Negroes (as they were then called), but completely accepting and respectful of them on a "one-on-one" basis. My dad's best friend, after Torkheild "Cap" Rieber (himself an anti-semite -- he had been ousted as chairman of Texaco in the late 1930s after selling aviation fuel to Hitler's Germany) was Milton Steinbach, chairman of Wertheim Co., an investment banking firm. The three of them would talk to the other two on the phone half-an-hour each day.

Similar was Dad's treatment of the two black porters at Cincinnati's suburban Norwood station, where his wife and sons would drop him off most Sunday evenings to travel east overnight on the Pennsylvania Railroad train. He couldn't have been more friendly with his banter or more generous with his tips to Walter, a short, older man, or Frank, a tall, young guy.

In truth, the author believes, given his choice, his father would have preferred to have spent his career as an officer in the U.S. Cavalry fighting the Indians out west in the 1870s and 1880s. He kept a couple of holstered "thirty-ought-six" rifles on either side of the fire place in Cincinnati and later in New York City. And he put together probably the finest collection of paintings by Henry Farney, lesser known, yet maybe better gifted, than his competitor, Frederick Remington (after Bud's death, the family gave his Farneys to the University of Wyoming in Laramie).

Dad, "Pop" we called him, was crazy for major-league baseball. Not the Reds -- in the 16 years my brothers and I lived in Cincinnati, he never, ever took us to Crosley Field -- but the New York Yankees. He had an absolute crush on their center fielder, Mickey Mantle.

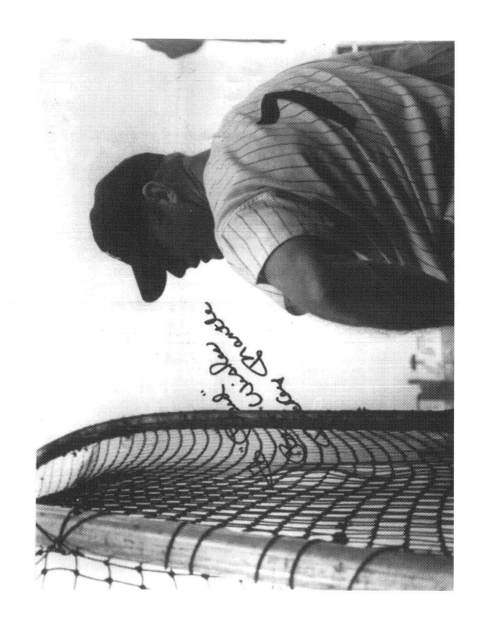

"NEW YORK, NEW YORK . . ."

Gordon, as seen elected a director of National City in the fall of 1923, was spending so much time on travel, phone calls and meetings concerning the bank that "one day Mr. Mitchell, the president, remarked: 'this man is working more for us than himself. Ask him if he will come here and take a position in the bank?'

"Mr. Rentschler gave up active management of the Rentschler companies and devoted his entire time to the bank. He was elected a vice-president and assistant to the president in 1925. Shortly thereafter the financial community began referring to him as 'Mitchell's heir apparent.'"[62]

Turning over management of the family companies had to have been difficult for Gordon, especially at H.O.R. (by way of constantly trying to reinvent itself now running trials on the largest diesel engine ever built in America). But Gordon had confidence in Bud, and he'd now brought into his companies Henry's boys just graduated from Princeton (Walter, at H.O.R., and Peter, at the foundry).

---

[62] David Lawrence, Gordon S. Rentschler obituary, The New York Times, March 15, 1948

Critically, as we have noted, Gordon's father was now dead -- it seems doubtful that Gordon would leave his dad, his businesses or his home-town while Adam lived!

Asked by a newspaper reporter "what had led him to give up the activities so well established and to turn to an entirely new business life, 'Mr. Mitchell!', he replied, with an admiring grin for the persuasive power of his boss. 'I decided, after Mr. Mitchell suggested it, that I might as well devote my full time to the bank. You see, after I became a director, I got so interested in the institution that I found myself commuting back and forth from Hamilton, spending at least half my time here."

Continued the story, "He is unmarried, his sister, Helen, running his home. This, incidentally, was purchased from Mr. Mitchell, who now occupies the larger one next door at No. 934 Fifth Avenue. For exercise both men follow the same course. Almost every morning they can be seen walking to work – down Fifth Avenue to Broadway, down Broadway to Wall Street, east two and a half blocks to the bank – it is a little more than four miles.

"To the interviewer, Rentschler's most striking characteristic is an intellectual curiosity which keeps him groping and probing for information on all manner of subjects." Asked what he enjoys most about the job, he replied: "Standing at the cross-roads of the world and watching everything that goes by. All a man could want is here and what isn't here can be observed from here. The commerce of the world, you know, flows through the offices of a great bank. From 55 Wall Street, studying people in their reactions to a great variety of condition, I have a telescope which comes pretty near sweeping the world."[63]

It hadn't taken Gordon and Helen long to leave Hamilton after their father died. Now he was on the east coast, Gordon dated Mary Coolidge Atkins, the Boston widow he'd met

---

[63] Lawrence Stern, The New York World, December 10, 1925

several years before at the Deeds' house in Dayton -- they were married in 1927. And Helen was betrothed the next year to Sidney D. Waldon, a British immigrant, who had been vice-president and general manager of Packard Motor Car Company before the war and Colonel Deeds' second-in-command of American aircraft production during the war, and they would live in Detroit.[64]

---

[64] Gordon and Mary would have three daughters, Phoebe (1928), Mimi (1929) and Susan (1933). Sidney and Helen produced a girl but she died at birth, never named (1929).

Built by Mitchell in 1925-26, the mansion at 934 Fifth Avenue is today the French Consulate of New York.

55 Wall Street, Headquarters, 1908–1961.

Gordon's office, 1926 – 1947, was at the headquarters of National City Bank, 55 Wall Street.

24

"JUST A 'JOB-SHOP'"

A case of "feast or famine", H.O.R. was an arsenal bristling with business in times of war but whistling for work in times of peace. As the decade of the Twenties unfolded, the challenge to fill the factories with profitable orders fell squarely on Bud, made president in 1925 when Gordon joined National City Bank.

The gigantic shops of H.O.R. sprawled across 25 acres north of downtown Hamilton, west of the Pennsylvania Railroad and east of the Baltimore & Ohio Railroad. Besides offices, the vast complex included a pattern shop, ferrous and non-ferrous foundries, machine shops, assembly bays, and even a special building for making crankshafts – truly, one of America's greatest manufacturing complexes.

Shifting from total concentration on marine engines during World War I, H.O.R. in the Twenties, after that brief surge of sugar-cane machinery, built five steel rolling-mills for Ford's huge new River Rouge factory between 1923 and 1927. Other products included automotive presses (e.g., for the new "turret"-type car roofs) and glass-making machinery.

Some dramatic new line of work needed, Bud pushed his company as hard as he could into manufacturing diesel engines, large ones, too. Accordingly, in May, 1924, he was licensed by Germany's M.A.N. (Maschinen-fabrik Augsburg-Nurnberg) to build their stationary and marine engines in

America under the "Hamilton" nameplate. The first engine made under this arrangement was shipped from Hamilton in 1926.The main market Bud targeted was power plants – five engines, for example, went into an electric utility in Vernon, California the next year.

Bud and his staff were doing considerable business in Europe whether with customers or licensors as indicated by a short note 12/26/26 to Helen, his sister, now living in New York City with Gordon: "The night before Christmas I gathered up the homeless foreigners from the shop – Germans, Danes and Swedes. Those northeners make a lot of this time of year. It was nice to have them around."[65]

In 1928 Bud merged H.O.R. with The Niles Tool Works to form the General Machinery Corporation. Niles was a long time supplier of gargantuan-size machine tools and "flag-ship" of an early conglomerate, Niles-Bement-Pond, now chaired by Colonel Deeds, who was dismembering the business (and, importantly as we shall see, looking for places to invest idle cash). Niles's shops sat on five acres west of General Machinery, between the B & O railroad and the river. While doing nothing to dampen the cyclicality of the Rentschler family's business, the merger gave General Machinery's engineers the ability to customize design and manufacture of equipment expressly for its finished products, e.g., a milling machine with 15'-wide ways (to make a naval gun turret) or a lathe with a length of 85' (to make a naval gun barrel) – those dimensions are not in error!

Bolstered by the addition of The Niles Tool Works, General Machinery "was a major reason why (Hamilton) could realistically claim to be the greatest manufacturing city of its size in the world and that more skilled artisans are to be

---

[65] Box 22, File 12, The Mary C. Rentschler Collection, New York Historical Society

found in Hamilton than any other city of its size in the world," according to Jim Blount, local historian.[66]

A nice complement. However, in reality, as suggested by the ironic selection of its first name, General Machinery never would create a substantial, dominant product-line. It was, and would remain, a vast, diverse "job shop". And that, in general, would be its undoing.

---

[66] Historical Collection at the Lane Library, Hamilton, Oho, Jim Blount, 2010

In a drive to diversify, General Machinery made "Hamilton" stamping presses to form "turret tops" for General Motors (circa 1937).

General Machinery tried to diversity in the Twenties with huge diesel engines (like these for a California electric utility)

…And turbines for dam projects in the western United States.

25

THE NEW YORK, NEW HAVEN & HARTFORD

Setting himself loose from Wright Aeronautical, Fred determined that he needed $1,250,000 to start his own aircraft-engine business and fund several months' production. These purposes would require equity capital, not debt, but he had no intention of trying to source the money from Wall Street after his experience with those investment bankers on the Wright board of directors, who had a "bland indifference . . . of the highly technical engineering problems that formed the basis of an aircraft engineering company."[67]

According to the official history of Pratt & Whitney (published in 1950), as regards arranging the company's initial financing, Gordon suggested to Fred that he present his plan to James K. Cullen, the president of Niles Bement Pond, whose headquarters were in New York City.

Continued the story: "Cullen and George A. Rentschler had been warm friends from the days of Frederick Rentschler's boyhood when Cullen, as president of the Niles Tool Works, operated next door to the Hooven-Owens-Rentschler company, headed by Mr. Rentschler, Sr., in Hamilton, Ohio."

---

[67] The Pratt & Whitney Aircraft Story, published by United Aircraft corporation, August, 1950, pg. 29

Cullen said "possibly Rentschler had come to the right place. Niles Bement Pond's Pratt & Whitney (machine tool) people (in Hartford) not only had idle money but idle space."[68] And, accordingly, a couple of days later, Fred took a New York, New Haven and Hartford train to Hartford to meet the management and tour the facilities.

The visit to Hartford, however, was academic. Fred already had his deal in hand, thanks to his brother Gordon. Now in and out of New York City on a frequent basis as the bank director, Gordon, given his industrial experience, in early 1924 also had been elected to the board of Niles Bement Pond.

The company was a very early "conglomerate", consisting of businesses building machine tools and related equipment, and, in the post-war era, possessing excess capacity and cash.

Colonel Deeds, nominated by Gordon, joined the Niles board in early 1925. Evidently dominating their new board (Deeds would become its chairman later that year), the two Ohioans arranged for the company to lend Fred the money he needed to start Pratt & Whitney Aircraft.[69]

[68] Ibid., pgs 16-17
[69] Pg. 316, Colonel Deeds: Industrial Builder, Isaac F. Marcosson, Dodds, Mead & Co., 1947

Pratt & Whitney factories in East Hartford, circa 1931

26

VROOOOOOM!

The stars got aligned over Fred in the fall of 1924. He was freed from his father's dismissive attitude toward aviation, from his directors' disinterest in their company, and from a mysterious debilitating illness. It was a good thing, too, because time was getting critical – those aircraft carriers were under construction!

Still living in New Jersey near the Wright factory, Fred early 1925 had got agreement to join him to form a new company from five key employees, most importantly its two top engineers, George Meade and Andy Wilgoos.[70] With Gordon arranging the financing, Pratt & Whitney Aircraft was launched that July, and the five men followed Fred to Hartford where they set up shop on Capitol Avenue in an abandoned Pratt & Whitney Machine Tool factory, from which they had to remove leaf tobacco grown for cigars,

Leaving aside each family's domestic challenges (finding a new home, moving furniture and belongings and settling into a new community), the work that was done in a short time in the new factory was mind-blowing -- designing components, procuring material, machining parts and testing engines. Especially complex to draft, source and inspect were three

---

[70] Mead is often cited as co-founding Pratt & Whitney with Fred, although The Pratt & Whitney Story, published by the parent company, United Aircraft Corp., in 1950, calls Fred "the founder". Pg. 4.

critically-differentiated components – a two-piece crankshaft, a two-piece forged crankcase and a one-piece master connecting rod.[71]

Fred had committed to the Navy he'd have an engine ready for them to test the next January. As if motivation for this group was needed, Colonel Deeds had promised each family involved in the start-up a turkey with trimmings if the internal deadline of Christmas was met. And it was, although the first crankcase was cast, not forged, and the first master connecting rod didn't arrive until December 23.[72]

While, by all measures, Wright Aeronautical was "the outstanding (airplane) engine company in the U.S. in 1925"[73], Pratt & Whitney impressively took over the lead the next year. Its engines demonstrated an up-to-now unreachably low ratio of weight-to-horsepower, exactly what the U.S. armed services -- not to mention the nascent commercial aircraft builders -- wanted. Bigger brother to the Wasp, the Hornet would debut just a year later.

The table below bench-marks the first two engine types from Pratt & Whitney -- the Wasp and the Hornet -- against the Lawrance (now Wright) J-5C that would propel Lindberg 33 hours across the Atlantic Ocean in March, 1927.

Builder	Model	Weight (Lbs.)	Horse-power	Lbs.HP
Wright	J-5C	600	223	2.9
P&W	Wasp	650	400	1.6
P&W	Hornet	750	525	1.4

The "name-of-the-game" being weight-to-power, the numbers make clear that the Wasp was an incredible advancement over the J-5C (and that the Hornet, introduced

---

[71] Pgs. 51-52, The Engines of Pratt & Whitney, Jack Connors, American Institute of Aeronautics and Astronautics, 2010

[72] Per Craig McBurney, consultant Pratt & Whitney Aircraft

[73] Pg. 26. The Pratt & Whitney Story

in 1927, was a further phenomenal improvement over the Wasp --- delivering 125 more horsepower but weighing just 100 lbs. more than its "older brother").

How far this industry had come since Kitty Hawk in 1903, when the engine in the Wright brothers' "Flyer" weighed 170 lbs. and produced 12 horse-power, a ratio of 14.2 Lbs/HP!

Pratt & Whitney built engines for Ford's Airplanes.

Powered with Pratt & Whitney's Hornet engines, Pan American Airways Sikorsky S-42s opened trans-oceanic service to the Orient and Europe.

27

'THE ROARING TWENTIES' PERSONIFIED

Over the balance of the decade, Mitchell amply lived up to the confidence the directors showed in 1921 when they'd appointed him head of National City Bank, although he'd never been a commercial banker. "Within less than two years Mitchell had accomplished a managerial 'tour de force'. The bank was back on its feet and moving forward."[74]

The decade of the Twenties provided Mitchell an ideal backdrop. Three events proved to be particularly advantageous: "the newly dominant role of the United States in the world economy, the emergence of New York City as the world's leading security market (and) the emergence of a large, well-to-do middle class in the United States."[75] A bright "up-and-comer", Mitchell would make the most out of the situation.

"Under Mitchell's leadership, the vision of an all-purpose financial intermediary became a reality," inclusive of a commercial bank, an investment bank, and a trust company, which had not occurred in America before. The latter was added to the corporation April 1, 1929 with the purchase of the Farmers' Loan and Trust Company. Mitchell's build-out now

---

[74] pg. 111, Citibank 1812-1970, Harold van B. Cleveland and Thomas F. Huertas, Harvard University Press, 1985

[75] Ibid. pg. 114

complete, the next day Gordon was promoted to presidency of National City Bank, with Mitchell as chairman overseeing the whole slew -- commercial bank, investment bank and new trust company.

Adding few executives at the top (Gordon was a rare exception) but culling out non-performers and installing a management compensation system, Mitchell ignited broad growth of the bank during the Twenties. As just one example, the number of National City's savings depositors between 1922 and 1929 sky-rocketed forty-fold from 6,300 to 232,000.[76]

In brief terms, when Mitchell became president in May, 1921, the institution was floundering. By decade's end, it was flourishing. Profits had risen from $900,000 in 1922 to $22.8 million in 1929. It not only had become the largest bank in the United States but also was challenging Britain's Midland Bank to be the largest bank in the world.[77]

A millionaire several times over now, the man, who'd sprung from a grungy Massachusetts town and worked the last two years of college to pay his tuition, began to enjoy life beyond the bank. As get-away places on weekends, in the early Twenties he, first, bought a huge seaside house for the summer time in Southampton, and, next, erected a massive home for the rest of the year in Tuxedo Park (75 miles northwest of the city) to which he'd commute -- Friday night up and Sunday night back -- by private parlor car on the Erie Railroad (in the author's eye, with uniformed bartenders mixing Martinis for him and his friends). And he wasn't done.

In 1925 and 1926, the Mitchells built a home in Manhattan -- a limestone mansion at 934 Fifth Avenue (between 74th and 75th Streets) that still stands. The five-story building was staffed

---

[76] Ibid. pg. 120
[77] Ibid, pgs. 134 and 157

with 15 "servants" to attend to the needs of the Mitchells and their two children and to accommodate the entertaining that his social position involved. (Today the structure is the French Consulate of New York.)

When the family took occupancy, the Mitchell's children, Rita (the mother of the author) and Craig, her brother, were 12 and 10, respectively.

28

LET THE GOOD TIMES ROLL

When the Mitchells moved into their luxurious new town house in late 1926, Gordon took up occupancy in the brownstone they had vacated next door, and he fetched Helen from Hamilton to supervise its staff. Some upgrade from 643 Dayton Street!

Gordon couldn't let go of Hamilton, though. He expanded and remodeled the modest family homestead he'd repurchased, converting it into a 17-room, 10,300 square foot mansion, including three fireplaces, a copper roof to capture rainwater in a cistern for household use, a three-car garage and two formal gardens. Occasions to use "The Farm" (as it became known) typically were business trips to "The Heartland."

After a year-or-so of courtship, Gordon was married in 1927 to Mary Coolidge Atkins, the now-widowed Boston lady he had earlier met at the Deeds' home. The next year Helen was betrothed to Sidney Dunn Waldon, Deed's second-in-command during the war, and they moved to Michigan.

Bringing a daughter, Faith, from her first marriage and wanting a family of their own, Mary and Gordon in 1928, for their main residence, bought a 20-room neo-Georgian style mansion on 25 acres in Locust Valley with luxuriant gardens and a dock on Long Island Sound -- not far, we suppose, from F. Scott Fitzgerald's mythical setting of The Great Gatsby. They produced three girls, Phoebe (1928), Mimi (1929) and Sue

(1933). Gordon, when not on business trips, would stay in the city during the week and go to Locust Valley for the weekends. The family would move back to Manhattan when the girls started grade school at Chapin

Fun times were had. For instance, Mary wrote a relative in Boston July of 1929 that "Charlie Mitchell and Sloan Colt arrived on Charlie's vessel, charted for the summer . . . and ate us out of house and home."[78] A frequent visitor, too, was Colonel Deeds who was made a director of National City Bank in 1928.

Setting an example for his fellow "farm boys" from Ohio on how to spend money in "The Gilded Age", Deeds built a huge yacht, launched mid-1930 and christened "Lotosland".

She was powered by two 500 horse-power diesel engines, measured 207' long and 28' wide, had a crew of 30 to care for guests in 9 staterooms (each with its own bathroom) who were delivered by a 5-passenger Pratt & Whitney-powered Sikorsky amphibious airplane, which perched atop the deck-house when not in use.[79]

As spectacular, if not more so, than what Gordon and the Colonel were doing, was the mansion built by Helen and Sidney Waldon. Living in Detroit (where he had many friends from the auto industry), they purchased 840 acres of land in Clarkston some thirty miles north, including (at 1,221') the highest point in south-eastern Michigan – from which they could see Lake Michigan to the west and Lake Huron to the east – and constructed a 19-room English-style house, which they called "Pine Knob".[80]

---

[78] Folder 11, Box 9, Mary C. Rentschler Collection, The New York Historical Society

[79] Pgs. 354-355, Colonel Deeds, Industrial Builder, Isaac F. Marcosson, Dodd, Mead & Co., 1947. Lotosland would be confiscated by the U. S. Navy in World War II.

[80] The mansion still stands and can be rented for special events, e.g., weddings.

Tragically, as Pine Knob was being built, Helen had a little girl who died at birth. Now nearly 40 years old, she would not have any more children. Sadly, too, the Waldons would live at Pine Knob just a decade, as we shall see.

29

PRATT GETS AIRBORNE,
THEN SOME . . .

Buoyed by the fact that the Wasp engine had passed its in-house test Christmas eve, Fred and Faye spent the New Year holidays with her family in Hamilton, but tragedy struck: their three-year old toddler, Jean, contracted a mysterious illness and died January 4, 1926. Pregnant again, Faye would never get over the loss of her first-born.[81]

Deeply saddened, too, Fred perforce had to have had his mind near totally occupied on the start-up of Pratt & Whitney Aircraft, indubitably one of the most amazing launches of a company in American history. Passing the Navy's stationary test on March 4, the Wasp was first flown on May 5, and the Navy in October ordered "production" engines to power 200 OS2U bi-planes that a friend of Fred, Chance Vought, was building for the two new aircraft carriers.[82]

The growth of the little company was explosive. By the next March (1927), Pratt & Whitney was shipping 15 Wasp engines per month, and the Hornet was coming on line. By that year's end, the original group of 33 employees had grown to over

---

[81] Letter from Ann Rentschler Cassidy to Headmaster, Renbrook School, September, 1992

[82] pg. 22, The Pratt & Whitney Aircraft Story, published by United Aircraft, August, . ("OS" stood for "Observation Scout")

800. The following August (1928) as the company celebrated its third birthday, with America's young aviation industry building more and more planes to fly people and mail, "commercial orders had pushed production to over 100 motors per month with demand still out-stripping supply."[83]

By 1929, Pratt & Whitney's Wasps and Hornets accounted for "more than 60% of the country's aircraft engine business . . . 90% of (its) commercial aircraft engine business, virtually all of the Navy's military aircraft . . . and a large share of the Army Air Corps airplanes."[84]

The original three-story, 3,000 square-foot building on Capital Avenue downtown long since inadequate, Fred and his team broke ground for a 400,000 square-foot, single-story building In East Hartford on July 16, 1929, almost four years to-the-day from the birth of Pratt & Whitney.

Completed in just under two years, the new plant and an adjacent airport, called Rentschler Field, were dedicated May 24-26, 1931. Leading the guests of honor were President Herbert Hoover and former President Calvin Coolidge, Other luminaries included General Douglas MacArthur, Charles Lindbergh, and Amelia Earhart. Also in attendance were Fred's three siblings and their wives, doubtlessly bursting with pride, plus Charles Lawrance.[85]

Sadly, though, while Fred would go on to greater and greater achievements, that dedication probably was the happiest moment of his career.

---

[83] pgs. 83, 110, Wings Over the World, Cary H. Mead, The Swannet Press, Wauwautosa, WI 1971

[84] pg.99, The Pratt & Whitney Story

[85] The program listed Lawrance as "President of the Aeronautical Chamber of Commerce"

30

PER ASPERA AD ASTRA

This chapter's title, translated "through hardships to the stars", seems a fitting way to sum up the next phase of Fred's career. Incredible as it sounds today, in early 1929, he sold Pratt & Whitney, not even four years old, to an aviation consortium formed by Bill Boeing, a young lumberman from the state of Washington who earlier had started up a company to build airplanes (remember, they first were made from spruce!).

Boeing's concept fifty years later would be called a "conglomerate". He purchased a gaggle of fledgling businesses spanning the young American aviation industry: other plane-makers (including Sikorsky, Vought and Northrop), airlines to carry people and mail (United and American) and an airfield in Los Angeles (LAX). And Boeing called his new firm United Aircraft & Transport Corporation.

Why would Fred sell his thriving company? He became president, reporting to Boeing, who was chairman. He diversified his holdings in aviation across a spectrum of businesses, seemingly all of which had high potential. And he became a multi-millionaire – the summer before the stock-market crash in October, 1929, Fred's holdings in United were worth $35 million and he took a profit of $9 million.[86]

That liquidity gave Fred and Faye the means to build a house of her, but not his, dreams. Since moving to Hartford,

---

[86] pg. 169, Fortune magazine, May 1934

they had lived in a couple of modest homes as preferred by Fred. Finally, the daughter of the hourly crane operator getting her way, she ordered built on 80 acres a colossal neo-Norman mansion, like one she had seen on Long Island (probably some weekend when Fred and she had flown over to Locust Valley to have lunch with Mary and Gordon). Built between 1930-1932, the house had 38 rooms (10 of them for "servants"), 14 bathrooms, a swimming pool, three tennis courts, a two-story living room 50 feet long by 25 feet wide, and a 6-car garage with heated parquet floors. With its cost totaling $1 million, the place was called Renbrook, "Ren," the first syllable of their surname, "brook", a rivulet the driveway crossed.

Meantime, the early Thirties would be as problematic for United Aircraft and Transport as the late Twenties had been promising for Pratt & Whitney. Compared with 1929, its inaugural year, revenues and profits in 1933 were down 40% and 80%, respectively:

UA&TC (12/31 year; millions)

	1929(a)	1933(b)
Revenue	$31.4	$19.6
Net Income	9.0	1.6

(a) company annual report (its first); (b) Fortune, May, 1934, pg. 88

The "top line" obviously was weighed down by factors affected by the country's economic collapse (e.g., fewer people flying). The "bottom line" additionally was freighted with the extra amortization from 60 new Boeing airplanes added to the fleet.

Operational worries, however, were nothing compared with political concerns. Upon the urging of the newly-elected President, Franklin D. Roosevelt, Congress passed the Airmail Act of 1934 that, while sounding innocent enough, forbade airlines from owning airplane manufacturers and vice-versa. As a consequence, United Aircraft & Transport Corporation was dissolved. Absolutely undone, Bill Boeing left the aviation industry for good. And Pratt & Whitney was spun off as, simply, United Aircraft Corporation, with Fred at his helm.

The average reader today would agree unhesitatingly with Roosevelt that airlines and their equipment suppliers should not have common ownership. But, for the rest of his life, Fred would neither forget nor forgive the Federal government for interfering in his business. The bottom had dropped out from under him, as it would twice again in his tenure at the helm of the engine company.

Writing some two decades later to his sister-in-law Mary (now Gordon's widow), Fred related: "We (e.g., Faye, his wife, and he) were cruelly hurt by Washington some twenty years ago . . . Faye and I were confused when our house came tumbling down over us. After fighting our way up from nothing and through uncharted seas, it was indeed a bitter pill. I think we both withdrew within ourselves more than ever and perhaps too much. But we did plan and fight on harder than ever . . ."[87]

---

[87] Folder 14, Box 12, May 21, 1953, Mary C. Rentschler Collection, The New York Historical Society

Fred conducts factory tour for President Roosevelt (circa 1939)

31

THE "WASH SALE"

The Great Depression, heralded by the Crash of October, 1929, rocked the United States and, of course, its biggest bank, National City. Profits dropped from a record in 1929 of $22.8 million to a loss in 1932 of $12.6 million.[88] Increasingly the country's economic collapse was blamed on practices of its bankers -- both commercial and investment -- and no one, of course, was more maligned than Mitchell, given his role as CEO of the nation's biggest bank.

His testimony before a committee of the U.S. Senate on February 21, 1933, uncovered the fact that he "had earned well over $1 million . . . in 1929 but had not paid any income tax that year because of a capital loss incurred in the sale of National City stock to his wife."[89] To give some scale to these numbers, the counsel to the committee, Ferdinand Pecora, was earning $255 a month and Senators, $9,000 per year.[90]

With anger but not remorse, we suppose, Mitchell resigned on February 26. The bank's board of directors choice as his replacement was not Gordon, though he had been groomed as Mitchell's successor, rather James H. Perkins, who had been

---

[88] Pg. 321, Citibank, 1812-1970, Harold van B. Cleveland and Thomas B. Huertas, Harvard University Press, 1985
[89] Ibid. pg. 185
[90] Pg. 147, The Hellhound of Wall Street, Michael Perino, The Penguin Press, 2010

running the trust business as a direct report to Mitchell and prior had had many years of commercial banking experience. That, indeed, Gordon, so closely associated with Mitchell, not only remained with the bank but also retained his position, appears attributable to the esteem in which he was held by both fellow officers and directors (especially Deeds, one would suspect) because of his democratic demeanor with all people and his genuine impact on the bottom-line.

On March 21 Mitchell was arrested at his home for tax evasion, and, to defend himself, he hired Max Steuer, "the greatest trial lawyer of his day." To raise the $100,000 retainer demanded by Steuer, Mitchell was so strapped for money, "he had to pass the hat among his friends . . ."[91] In his subsequent trial, "Mitchell testified that he had acted in good faith," relying on his lawyers who "told him that the tax transaction (with his wife) was perfectly legal . . . (that he) had engaged in perfectly legitimate 'tax avoidance', not illegal 'tax evasion."[92]

Reflective of the national ground-swell against "banksters", whose fury was fed by Roosevelt just taking office, Congress signed on May 27 the Glass-Steagall Act, that mandated the separation of commercial banks and investment banks. At National City, "gone was talk of a financial department store and investment banking powerhouse."[93]

Perkins, meanwhile, "took steps to disassociate the institution from Mitchell. Bank officers and directors were apparently advised to have no contacts with Mitchell."[94] He'd lost everything.

"In 1938, the U.S. Supreme Court ruled that (Mitchell) owed $1.1 million in back taxes and penalties. He could have declared bankruptcy, but claimed it wasn't the 'square thing' to do. He eventually paid off everything he owed . . . although

---

[91] Ibid. pg .297
[92] Pg.193, Citibank
[93] Ibid. pg.227
[94] Ibid.pg.192

he lost the Fifth Avenue mansion and the other houses to foreclosures."[95]

In the meantime (1935), Mitchell had become chairman of Blyth & Co., a here-to-fore West-coast investment banker. If never able to redeem himself ethically, Mitchell was able to recover financially by operating on a national, indeed international scale. In this regard, his prime accomplishment was positioning Blyth as the lead underwriter in the first-ever public offering of the shares of Ford Motor Company launched a month after his death in January, 1956.

---

[95] Ibid. pg.298. He lived the remainder of his life at #1 Sutton Place South, New York City. His wife, Elizabeth, preceded him in death in 1953.

Renbrook, the 41-room mansion that Faye and Fred built in Hartford between 1930-1932

32

HIS WINGS CLIPPED

Where, as we have seen, Roosevelt had truncated Gordon's bank in 1933 with the Glass-Steagall Act, the president also clipped the wings of Fred's aerospace company in 1934 with the Air Mail Act. Sadly, it was a cloud that Fred would not allow himself to walk out from under the rest of his life. Business for him must have become, per the cliché, "one damn thing after another." Ironically, though, in our view the edict from Washington became a main motivator, in our estimation.

He admitted as much nearly two decades later in a letter to his sister-in-law, Mary: "Faye and I were confused when our own house comes tumbling down over us. After fighting our way up from nothing and through uncharted seas, it was indeed a bitter pill. I think we both withdrew within ourselves more than ever and perhaps too much. But we did plan and fight on harder than ever."[96]

Refocused on Hartford operations after the break-up of the Boeing conglomerate in 1934, Fred's biggest problem at Pratt & Whitney was management -- top-management, at that. George Mead, sometimes cited as the business's co-founder, not only refused Fred's invitation to become president of the new United Aircraft, but also, equally hurtful, opposed Fred's

---

[96] Folder14, Box 12, May 21, 1953, Mary C. Rentschler Collection, The New York Historical Society

next choice, Don Brown, who, anyways, got and held the position until his untimely death in 1940.

Plagued with health issues, Mead would hang around until 1939 when he retired. Nominally head of R&D, Mead seems to have projected a "persona" larger than that and thus destabilized an organization that ceaselessly fathomed and whispered what power he exerted. Like Fred, with money from the 1929 IPO, Mead had built a mansion that may further have added to the mystery around this man. Meantime, very serious technical problems affected the bearings Pratt & Whitney was using, and one wonders if top-management tension could partly be blamed for not fixing the issue in a more timely manner.

Then, too, competition was heating up. Wright Aeronautical, Fred's "alma mater", had merged in 1929 with Curtiss Aeroplane to form Curtiss-Wright, and, suddenly, Pratt & Whitney had real competition. In fact, by 1935 Pratt & Whitney's "tremendous lead (was) completely dissipated in terms of both military and commercial engines."[97]

But war was on the horizon and would transform Fred's business.

---

[97] Pg. 46, The Engines of Pratt & Whitney, Jack Connors, American Institute of Aeronautics and Astronautics, 2010

"...EVERYTHING
BLOOMING"

Always the "alpha male" (as we have seen), Gordon had been solicitous about the well-being of his younger siblings since he first donned long trousers.

Where we have related how Perkins, the new chairman of National City Bank. had ordered its officers to steer clear of Mitchell after his embarrassing resignation, Gordon evidently kept in touch with his old boss, albeit discreetly.

Thus it so happened that Gordon introduced his youngest brother, Bud, to Mitchell's only daughter, Rita -- we assume sometime in 1934. She was just 20 years old, while he more than twice her age, 42. Evidently a bachelor for some time (Joan having left him, probably when Prohibition was ended in 1933), Bud got officially divorced and, on November 11, 1936, he and Rita were united by a Catholic priest in her parents' apartment in the presence of just a handful of guests (including Gordon and Mary and their three small daughters).

We get a glimpse of the newly-weds' life from a letter Gordon wrote to Mary the following summer (1937) on one of his periodic visits to Ohio, which typically included stops at General Machinery in Hamilton and the Miami Conservancy District in Dayton.

"Rita and Bud seemed to have everything blooming" (perhaps a sly inference his new sister-in-law was four months pregnant with her first child, George, Jr.). "Rita is running her little house very nicely. They have found an extremely good cook and a very satisfactory maid and between them did more than give me the three square meals while I was there. I slept at the old farm."

In regards to General Machinery, Gordon continued, "Bud's things are coming along in splendid shape. In fact, everything at the shop looked well. They have two enormous presses going through for General Motors which will be used for making Buick and Chevrolet bodies. These are two of the biggest ones they have ever built and show up very well in the shop. The Niles building is full of railroad tools and special equipment going through and, of course, the Diesel shop is in excellent condition with plenty of work.

"So with the corn growing and the shops full, everything in Butler County looks rosy."[98]

George, Jr. would arrive that December, and, in August, 1939, twin boys, Frederick Brant Rentschler II and Charles E. Mitchell Rentschler (the author of this book, of course!). In 1941 Bud, Rita and their three sons would move 20 miles south to Cincinnati whose schools they believed were better than those in Hamilton. For $10,000 they purchased a large house built by a widow but left two years empty because she'd dreamt she'd die if she moved in. With a panoramic view of the Ohio River, the home years later (after the Rentschlers had moved East) would form the backdrop for the opening scene of the movie "Rainman".

---

[98] Box 10, File 4, letter from Gordon S. Rentschler, 8/23/37 Mary C. Rentschler Collection, The New York Historical Society

34

A WELCOME INTERLUDE?

That Gordon was not fired when Mitchell resigned in February, 1933 oddly might represent the high point of his career. Since joining the bank in 1925, Gordon had been seen as Mitchell's constant understudy and eventual successor, both by outsiders and insiders.

The board of directors' decision to leave Gordon in his job as president under Perkins is testament to their high regard for him, his business acumen, his integrity, his drive, but, above all, his thoughtful, kindly way with people -- and people of every income-level, creed and color.

In some respects, National City would be an easier business to run after Mitchell's departure. The Cuban sugar interests (which had taken up loads of management time) were written off in 1933. And the investment banking division, in keeping with the terms of the Glass-Steagall Act, was liquidated in 1934.

Yet as the Great Depression kept its tight grip on America's economy until the coming of World War II, businesses typically were not looking to borrow new money from banks. Additionally, people were less inclined to leave their savings in banks --the Federal government had enacted deposit insurance which neutered their reputation for safety and had imposed ceilings on interest rates which limited their ability to compete.[99]

With unusual courage and foresight, Perkins and Gordon cut staff sparingly and kept branch offices open. After recording losses of $85.3 million (including write-offs, of course) in 1931 and 1934, National City earned cumulative profits of $67.8 million between 1935-1940.[100]

Gordon appreciated, too, no doubt, that being eight years younger than Mitchell, under normal circumstances, he would have had to wait that long to succeed him. In any event, he had a prodigious work-load as a director of several prestigious corporations, including Anaconda Copper, Union Pacific Railroad, Home insurance, and United Aircraft, while also a trustee of Princeton University and the Massachusetts Institute of Technology.

Maybe most important of all, Perkins' becoming Chairman gave Gordon more time to spend with his wife and three daughters, who he'd moved from Locust Valley to an apartment opposite Central Park on Fifth Avenue when the oldest girl, Phoebe, started school at Chapin in 1936.

[99] pg. 303, Citibank, 1812-1970, Harold van B. Cleveland and Thomas F. Huertas, Harvard University Press, 1985
[100] Ibid. pg. 321

CALL TO WAR

United Aircraft & Transport, its former parent, dismembered by Washington, and Pratt & Whitney, itself, strained by a trifecta of issues -- dissension at the top, supplier quality problems and vastly improved competitors, Fred by the fall of 1938 faced a decline in engine orders so deep that there seemed a "likelihood that the entire plant would have to close."[101] The Thirties had been as grim, for Fred, as the Twenties, glorious.

Suddenly, though, in the fall of 1939, the French government ordered so many engines that Pratt & Whitney not only dedicated 150,000 square feet of existing floor space but also rushed to add on 280,000 contiguously. The next autumn, the British followed suit with so much business that Fred built them their own 425,000 square foot building, alongside one 375,000 already in place, meaning that Pratt & Whitney, in less than three years, had provided the U.S.' main allies 1,230,000 square feet of space solely dedicated to production of engines for them.[102]

Most importantly, Fred straightened out his top management team. After Mead's retirement and Brown's demise, Fred in 1940 put himself back in charge as chairman of the board and appointed Jack Horner, president, Bill Gwinn, assistant to the

---

[101] pg. 127, the Pratt & Whitney Aircraft Story, published by the company, 1950

[102] Ibid., pg. 133

president, and Luke Hobbs, chief engineer, the group that led the company during the war.

By June 30, 1942, Pratt & Whitney's East Hartford facilities had grown to 2.7 million square feet – and it was not sufficient. So three satellite plants with another 2.6 million square feet were built nearby in New England, and, in 1943, an engine factory, duplicative of East Hartford with 3.0 million square feet, was opened in Kansas City, Missouri, strategically placed far enough inland to escape possible ravages of enemy bombers.[103] In addition, Pratt & Whitney licensed America's car manufacturers to build its aircraft engines. Construction of the factories, of course, was just the beginning, as these facilities had to be equipped for machining, welding, heat-treating, assembling, testing, etc., and tens of thousands of workers recruited and trained. In fact, Pratt & Whitney's workforce during the war climbed from 3,000 to 40,000.

By war's end, August, 1945, Fred's company and its licensees had powered 50% of the horsepower for the planes of America's armed services, which included not just fighters but also bombers and cargo planes. And it wasn't only the number of engines but their power – by early 1945 Pratt & Whitney engines used in combat had over 3,000 horsepower.[104] Remember, just twenty years before, the first Wasp had produced just 400 horsepower.

While Fred was rapidly expanding his business in the early 1940's, he conversely was down-sizing the Renbrook mansion. About one-third got torn down in 1941-42, the reasons reported including a rise in local property taxes, a shortage of staff gone to war work, and Fred's discomfort with the grandiosity of the place.

---

[103] Ibid., pg. 137
[104] Ibid., pg. 143

One of the 2,751 Liberty Ships Built in World War II

36

"GIVE ME LIBERTY . . .!"

While Fred was making an unparalleled contribution to the Allied war effort in the air, Bud was doing his level best to defeat the Axis powers on the seas. Early in 1941, the British government gave General Machinery an order to produce a prototype steam engine for a cargo vessel (to be called a "Liberty ship") that might be built in U.S. shipyards faster than German U-boats could sink them. Soon after, the U.S. Maritime Commission issued contracts to 13 other American companies to also make these metric-based engines, though designating General Machinery as the design agent and production lead.

Bud's brother-in-law, Sidney Waldon, had a big role in helping General Machinery land this contract and start its production. Being English, he was fully versed with the metric system and had had years of experience in automotive manufacture. In fact, at the outset of hostilities he and Helen moved to Gordon's farm in Hamilton so that he could work for Bud at General Machinery where he was made a vice-president and a director. (Sidney would die at war's end in Hamilton in 1945.)[105]

That the engines, being steam, theoretically were obsolete was not the point: they were easy to build and easy to maintain.

---

[105] Helen and Sidney never would return to live at Pine Knob, which they gave Ford Hospital which used it to rehabilitate wounded soldiers during the war and purchased it outright in 1950.

They were 23' high, 17' wide and 32' long, and weighed 144 tons[106], and each was sent in sections on five flat-cars (reminiscent of those disassembled Corliss engine-generators shipped Ford Motor Company three decades earlier!) to one of a dozen shipyards on either coast of the U.S.

Dubbed "the shopping basket" of World War II, the Liberty ship was 441' long. While possessing a top speed of just 11 knots, it could haul 440 tanks or 2,840 Jeeps or several hundred mules, or just about anything else needed. Astonishingly, only 195 of the 2,751 lumbering ships were lost during World War II.[107] Astoundingly, two-thirds of the cargo that left the U.S. during the war was carried by Liberty ships![108]

If production had been spread evenly, each of those 14 vendors would have supplied 7% of the engines for Liberty ships. General Machinery, however, by November, 1943, was completing and shipping an engine every day, and, by war's end, had built 826, or 31 %, of the engines for Liberty ships, way more than any other builder. Amazingly, its workforce, swollen now to some 4500 people, consisted totally of women and men over 40 years – the younger males gone off to the armed services.

General Machinery was also making humongous-size milling machines for America's naval yards, and a subsidiary in West Virginia was producing enormous gun barrels for its naval vessels. Think of war-time General Machinery as a smaller American version of Germany's Krupp (minus the slave labor, of course!).

---

[106] Pg. 70, The Diesel Builders, John Kirkland, Interurban Press, Glendale CA, 1985

[107] Jim Blount Collection, 2010, Layne Library, Hamilton, Ohio

[108] Web-site of San Francisco-based SS Jeremiah O'Brien, one of only two surviving Liberty ships. The O'Brien has its original General Machinery engine that, well-maintained by volunteers, periodically pushes the ship on excursions around the Bay.

In recognition of its efforts, General Machinery received the Army and Navy "E" and the Maritime "M", the first company in America to win the awards.[109] And, as if he hadn't had enough to deal with during the war, Bud organized a company to construct and manage a shipyard in Savannah, Georgia, which itself built 83 Liberty ships.[110]

[109] Obituary, May 23, 1972, The Hamilton (Ohio) Journal
[110] Pg. 34, The General Machinery Corp., 1845-1945, Sidney D. Waldon, Wm. E. Rudge's Sons, Inc., New York, N.Y. 1945

GENERAL MACHINERY LAYOUT 1

GENERAL MACHINERY LAYOUT 2

Liberty Ship slips down ways at Savannah Georgia's
shipyard, a subsidiary of General Machinery
— 83 were built here in World War II.

General Machinery workers with the last of the Liberty Ship engines they built in World War II.

General Machinery's effort during World War II included
extraordinarily long lathes for boring gun barrels for the U.S. Navy.

37

"... A SERVANT OF THE PEOPLE"

Gordon was thrust into the chairmanship of National City Bank when James H. Perkins, Mitchell's successor, died unexpectedly in 1940.

His tenure would last just eight years, or until 1948, when on March 3, he, too, suddenly passed away on a business trip to Havana.

Profits during Gordon's tenure were good, averaging $28.3 million per year, compared with $13.5 million between 1935-1939 on Perkins' watch (this excludes 1934, Perkins' first year in the job, which recorded a deficit of $58.1 million due to extraordinary losses from divesting the Cuban interests and closing the investment banking division). The company's official history explains: "The bank's profits during the war years were excellent, yet came from helping the Treasury finance the war, rather than returns from assuming credit and interest-rate risks – the normal business of a commercial bank."[111]

Post-war results were strong, too. The bank's loans to consumers more than tripled between June, 1945 and June, 1948. And Gordon had advised the shareholders at the start

---

[111] pg. 215, Citibank, 1812-1970, Harold van B. Cleveland and Thomas F. Huertas, Harvard University Press, 1985

of that year "so far as industrial activity and employment are concerned, the immediate prospect could hardly be more satisfactory."[112]

Gordon's success as a banker seems to have emanated from two things. First, he was an "industrialist as a banker". He could unusually relate to the top management of his customers, because he had been "one of them" – he'd run real businesses! One of Gordon's outside directors, John Neylan, wrote him in early 1944: "I do not have to tell you what a cordial and warm feeling there is . . . toward the bank as the result of the top officers getting out here, meeting and knowing the crowd and having an understanding of the situation . . . you could not have spent $500,000 in advertising and have accomplished the good . . . that flowed from the visits here during the last ten years . . ."[113] Gordon himself particularly enjoyed "barnstorming" by train across the country (my father called it "drumming"), talking up his bank with CEOs – and, of course, occasionally catching his breath by watching the Herefords on "The Farm" in Hamilton.

The ultimate reason for his success, though, was his interest in, and kindness to, people of all types. Here we quote from his obituary written by David Lawrence, a columnist for The New York Evening Post, who was in the class behind Gordon at Princeton and thus knew him over four decades:

". . . known to relatively few Americans, (Gordon Rentschler) played a significant part in the economic life of America . . . (His) advice to government was always given with the deepest sincerity because he believed thoroughly that private finance and government operations were not incompatible . . . (his) advice to private industry was blunt and realistic. Many an industrialist came to him to discuss problems of the day. He was a busy man but he gave himself to others . . . that in the end

---

[112] Ibid, pg. 218
[113] Ibid, pg.216

broke down his health . . . (He) was a man never too busy to worry about individual employees in his large organization . . . He built up the National City Bank to be the largest bank in the largest city in the world . . . He was a servant of the people as much as any man who served in public office."[114]

Gordon was buried in the family plot in Hamilton (where Mary also would be interned when she died in 1988). And Fred was elected to the board of the bank in Gordon's stead.

---

[114] March 5, 1948, The New York Evening Post

TOUR DE FORCE

With just a fraction of the workers left from building engines for Liberty ships and other military product, General Machinery decided post-war to remold its business around furnishing diesel power for locomotives. As seen the company for years had been making diesels, predominantly, though, for power plants and naval ships.

Diesel locomotives had begun to appear in the Thirties when both General Motors and General Electric entered the business with fresh designs and ample capital. The three much smaller steam locomotive producers, Baldwin, American and Lima, in order of their size, seemed far less interested in embracing the new diesel technology than squeezing that last bit of power out of a tender full of coal.

Deciding to buy his way into the locomotive business, Bud set his sights on Lima located in the town of Lima, Ohio, 120 miles north of Hamilton, and, like General Machinery, on the main-line of the Baltimore & Ohio Railroad. Of significance, as seen later, Lima also produced power shovels and cranes.

On October 1, 1947, in a friendly transaction between two public companies, the larger one, Lima, "bought its new partner (General Machinery) via an exchange of stock," giving the former 58% of the shares versus 42% for the latter, and the new firm was called Lima-Hamilton Corporation. It, however, became "soon apparent that the Rentschlers were in firm control" since Bud (who had been chairman of General Machinery) was made chairman of the new company.

Bud got right down to business. The concept was Hamilton would build the diesel engines, Lima, the rest of the locomotive. And Lima-Hamilton shipped 111 locomotives in 1949 and 1950, ominously most of them switch engines of 1200 horse-power, for yard use, as opposed to "road" locomotives of 2500 horse-power or greater, for long distances.[115]

Bud, however, wasn't done, as he next turned his sights on Baldwin, which was situated on the Pennsylvania Railroad in Eddystone, Pennsylvania, mid-way between Philadelphia and Wilmington. While Baldwin had first built diesels there in 1925, its production facilities, executives' mind-set and employees' skills were still focused on steam.[116] More than twice the size of the former General Machinery's Hamilton site, with ferrous and non-ferrous foundries, huge machine shops and assembly buildings, as well as a 6-story office, the Eddystone complex was so well-equipped and so vast it had built and shipped steam locomotives down the Delaware River to the Allies at the rate of one per day during World War II. It was not until the conflict ended that Baldwin got serious about building diesel locomotives.

A case of "'déjà vu' all over again", three years later, in November, 1950, a larger Baldwin Locomotive bought smaller Lima-Hamilton through an exchange of stock, with Baldwin's share-holders receiving 57% of the ownership and Lima-Hamilton's, 43%. A clear sign that, once again, he had master-minded the deal and had taken control, Bud became chairman of the board and chief executive officer of the new

---

[115] pgs. 236 and 237, Lima, The History, Eric Hirsimaki, Hundman Publishing Inc., 1986

[116] Samuel M. Vauclain, long-time president of Baldwin Locomotive, had declared "the power of the early diesel prototypes was inferior to steam." Pg. 392, Vauclain, G.A. Crimmins, Rutledge Printing, Oakland Park, Ill., 2011

company, called Baldwin-Lima-Hamilton Corporation, which at year's end employed about 14,000 people.

In effecting this merger, Bud became the third brother in his family to head a corporation listed on the New York Stock Exchange (something that had never happened before and hasn't happened since). Its symbol was "B".

That terribly vexing question, though, still haunted Bud: could he establish a viable, on-going business that could survive the immutable cycles of capital goods manufacturing?

HIS GREATEST
ACHIEVEMENT

In regard to Fred Rentschler, Colonel Deeds stated in his memoirs: "Next to the Wright Brothers, he has probably, in his quiet way, done as much or more for aviation than any other one man."[117] Deeds was referencing, first, creating Pratt & Whitney Aircraft in 1925, and, second, supplying 85% of the engines for Allied aircraft in World War II[118]

Left out, because Deeds' biography was published in 1947, was Fred's third contribution to aviation: development of the United States' first jet aircraft engine, which was completed in 1950 and got him on the cover of Time magazine, May 28, 1951, with the story entitled: "Mr. Horsepower".

In some ways, this last achievement seems the most stunning of the three. Pratt & Whitney's production of piston engines "was so important (at the outset of World War II) that the Government arbitrarily ruled it out of experimenting with jets: it did not want anything to interfere with engine and plane output."[119].

---

[117] pg. 320, Colonel Deeds: Industrial builder, Isaac P. Marcosson, Dodd, Mead & Company, 1947

[118] pg. 143, The Pratt & Whitney Story, published by the company, 1950

[119] Time magazine, May 28, 1951

Fred had completely acceded to the U.S. Government's insistence, and, as a consequence, had NO gas turbines for sale when peace came.

Yet domestic competitors, licensed by European suppliers, had jet engines and a five-year head-start. And the military market for piston engines had dried up by this time. The migraines of the mid-late Thirties had to have returned for Fred.

Undaunted, though, Fred and his team plunged ahead. Pratt & Whitney in 1947 bought the rights to a Rolls-Royce jet engine, with the proviso it could make any changes it wanted. It did, and, in four years, was producing its first jet engine, for both military and commercial uses.

There was, unhappily, a lot of sadness in Fred's last few years. Faye and he moved to Florida, in 1950, because of her declining health. They'd bought a "guest house" on the grounds of the Boca Raton Racquet and Beach Club, where Fred played tennis daily. She passed away in 1953.

Plagued by lung and other issues caused by a life-time of heavy cigarette smoking, Fred suffered, too, those last years and passed away in Florida in May, 1956. He was buried in Hartford next to his wife and their first daughter, Jean.

The following year her sisters donated Renbrook to a private grade school that bears its name today.

TIME

THE WEEKLY NEWSMAGAZINE

UNITED AIRCRAFT'S RENTSCHLER
"The engine is the key to air supremacy."

May 28, 1951

40

TOO LITTLE, TOO LATE

Prospects seemed excellent for the newly-formed Baldwin-Lima-Hamilton, given the boom underway both in the locomotive and construction equipment businesses. Locomotive manufacturing was moved from Lima to Eddystone to make room to build more shovels and cranes, while non-engine items, like turbine wheels for dams, were shifted from Hamilton to Eddystone to provide space to make more diesel engines. Meantime, evidence of its broad capability, Eddystone was casting four manganese-bronze propellers, weighing 30 tons each, for the new super-liner, United States, being built for United States Lines, on whose board Bud sat. The factory also produced forging presses, including a 50,000-ton machine still punching out aerospace parts for the highly-profitable Wyman-Gordon division of Precision Castparts, one of Warren Buffet's most-prized acquisitions.

With a New York Stock Exchange ticker symbol of "B", BLH got off to a strong start. First, the initial round of dieselization of American railroads, which had begun in 1946, became so strong in the early 1950s that, even though the leaders, General Motors and General Electric, armed with fresh product and strong balance sheets, grabbed big chunks of the market, there were still plenty of orders left for the smaller competitors, BLH, American Locomotive and Fairbanks-Morse. And second, the interstate highway program, launched by President Dwight

D. Eisenhower, who had seen first-hand the value of the Autobahn to Hitler's Germany, caused a boom for the U.S. construction equipment business and, thus, Lima.

Net Profits (mills.)—12/31 years

1951	$4.6	1954	$4.0
1952	7.2	1955	1.8
1953	7.4	1956	6.4

BLH set up its corporate office in New York City, and Bud and Rita moved there in 1956 after the death of her father whose apartment they took over.

Unfortunately, the "bottom line" was deceiving. The locomotive business, the core of Bud's strategy, had collapsed by mid-decade with U.S. railroads completing their first round of dieselization. In fact, BLH's loss on locomotives was so great it abandoned the business in 1956. Eddystone soldiered on with non-railroad business, but Hamilton, shorn of its major diesel-engine customer, was closed in 1960 (the property -- 30 acres of shops and offices – sold to Champion Paper).

The next several years for BLH were difficult, as shown by the numbers:

Net profits (mills) – 12/31 years

1957	$3.0	1961	$1.4
1958	4.6	1962	1.9
1959	5.0	1963	1.0
1960	1.3		

Unintentionally, BLH had become an amalgam of its non-locomotive businesses -- construction machinery, specialty electronics, rolling mills, automotive presses, etc., a "conglomerate", ironic in that the day of "multi-industry" companies had just dawned. It was, however, a large business.

With 7,000 employees, down from 14,000 at its inception in 1950, its 1961 sales of $123 million put BLH #335 on the "Fortune 500" list (by comparison, that year Cummins Engine had revenues of $136 million and ranked #309).

Remaining independent did not seem sensible to Bud. Merger talks with Lockheed Aircraft had collapsed after the crash of its much-heralded Electra prop-jet airplane. So, in July, 1965 (Bud was 72) BLH was sold to Armour & Co., meat-packer-turned-conglomerate, on whose board he had sat for a dozen years. Armour proceeded to break apart BLH and, itself, was purchased in May, 1970, and subsequently dismantled, by the Greyhound Corporation.

Bud died peacefully, aged 79, in New York City, 1972, and is buried, next to my mother, in the Mitchell plot in South Hampton, N.Y.

Louisville & Nashville 2-8-4 (1948)

Last steam locomotive built in Lima, Ohio, 1948

First diesel locomotive built in Lima, Ohio 1950

Even with such a locomotive, Baldwin-Lima-Hamilton could
not catch up to General Motors and General Electric.

Making huge "one-off" aerospace projects could not near fill the void left at Eddystone after locomotive manufacture was discontinued.

Bud in his New York office (Circa 1958)

ABOUT THE AUTHOR

Born in 1939 in New York City, I was raised with a twin brother and an older brother in Cincinnati, Ohio. While I was only in grade school, I got hooked on a career in manufacturing. I reveled in the sights, sounds and smells of the machine shops my paternal grandfather, had founded and father now ran in Hamilton (twenty miles north) and delighted in the ride on an 800-horsepower diesel "switch engine" made in Lima (eighty miles further north) at a business "Pop" bought in 1947. But, while I'd had summer jobs during college (Princeton University) at Lima and at Eddystone, Pa., the home of Baldwin Locomotive my father had acquired in 1950 to form Baldwin-Lima-Hamilton Corporation (somewhere in the middle of the Fortune 500 list), its future by this point seemed precarious. In fact, it was sold to Armour & Co. in 1965, and broken apart.

So, after serving in the U.S. Marine Corps, attending Harvard Business School, working on Wall Street, consulting for McKinsey & Co., and learning something about manufacturing management at a couple of mid-sized companies, I joined Cummins (then) Engine in 1976 in the production arena, as close a fit as I could find to my ancestral business.

Truthfully, I'd had a desire to work at Cummins since I'd watched their engines being installed in Lima shovels that summer years ago.

After seven years, though, I left Cummins because the sole surviving business started by Adam, The Hamilton Foundry & Machine Co., had gone into Chapter XI, so I dove in to see what

I could do. Despite our two plants being unionized and our customers buying more and more castings from Mexico and China, we improved profits ten years in a row. And we bought three more foundries. Our biggest customer, not surprisingly, was Cummins. However, foreign competition (and, frankly, my own optimism) proved too much and we filed for bankruptcy in 1997.

During these times I served as a director of a couple of publicly-owned businesses: Hurco Cos., machine-tool builder, Indianapolis, IN; and Accuride Corporation, maker of truck wheels, Evansville, IN.

Subsequently, I have spent much of my time writing. At Princeton I had served as managing editor of the daily newspaper and written an honors thesis for the History Department. So, I spent a dozen years (from 1998 to 2010) doing research on Wall Street, covering machinery companies, e.g., Caterpillar, Deere, Cummins, etc., until age 70. Then, I turned to doing biography, first, The Cathedral Builder, the life of J. Irwin Miller, CEO of Cummins, patron of the arts, religious leader and philanthropist, and, now, FORTITUDE, the story about my ancestors.

I have gotten ceaseless encouragement from Suzie, my wife, as well as consistent support from our three children, Adam, Charlie and Marie, and their spouses, Mary-Kate, Mary and Peter. May they, as well as their children, our grandchildren, be endowed with the fortitude of our forbearers!

Charles E. Mitchell guiding his name-sake and grandson, Charles E. Mitchell Rentschler
(Author of the Biography)

(author of biography)

Printed in the United States
By Bookmasters